W9-BWL-550

Searching *for* Thoreau

If you have a home computer with Internet access you may:
- request an item to be placed on hold.
- renew an item that is not overdue or on hold.
- view titles and due dates checked out on your card.
- view and/or pay your outstanding fines online (over $5).

To view your patron record from your home computer click on Patchogue-Medford Library's homepage: **www.pmlib.org**

Henry David Thoreau in 1856 daguerreotype

Searching *for* Thoreau

On the Trails and Shores of Wild New England

Tom Slayton

Images from the Past
Bennington, Vermont

Cover photographs by Bridget Besaw. Front: West Branch of the Penobscot River, Maine; Back: Katahdin Lake, Maine

Illustrations by Ethan Slayton

Author photograph by David Goodman

All rights reserved under International and Pan-American Copyright Conventions. No part of this book may be reproduced in any form or by any electronic, photographic, or mechanical means, including information storage and retrieval systems, without permission in writing from the publisher

Library of Congress Cataloging-in-Publication Data

Slayton, Tom, 1941-
  Searching for Thoreau : on the trails and shores of wild New England / Tom Slayton.
    p. cm.
  Summary: "Ten essays that interweave the author's first-hand experiences and those of the great American writer/naturalist Henry David Thoreau with their respective reflections on the importance of preserving wild places and the causes of change"--Provided by publisher.
  Includes bibliographical references.
  ISBN 978-1-884592-44-7 (pbk.)
  1. Thoreau, Henry David, 1817-1862--Knowledge--New England. 2. Thoreau, Henry David, 1817-1862--Influence. 3. Natural history--New England. 4. New England--In literature. 5. Environmental protection in literature. 6. Transcendentalism (New England) I. Title.

  PS3057.N44S43 2007
  818'.309--dc22

                    2007034263

ISBN 1-884592-44-9 paperback

Copyright ©2007 Tom Slayton

First edition, First printing

Published by Images from the Past, Inc.
www.imagesfromthepast.com
PO Box 137, Bennington VT 05201
Tordis Ilg Isselhardt, Publisher

Design and Production: Toelke Associates, Chatham, NY

Printed in the USA

Printer: Versa Press, Inc., East Peoria, IL

This book is for Elizabeth

Contents

Foreword

Wise Travel

Travel through the wilds made Thoreau buoyantly happy," Tom Slayton remarks in his introduction. Thoreau was a Romantic. He believed in the goodness of life: "Surely joy is the condition of life." He was a roamer, too. "I have traveled a good deal in Concord," he wrote—an emphasis on local exploration that surprised readers of *Walden*. He suggested that we pass through our native village as if we were in another country. He wanted us to be in place, in peace; not transient, scattered. How can you go about your hometown like this? He showed us how.

He embraced nature and culture fully, intimately, in all seasons, all weathers. He wanted direct contact with his home ground. To take in his environment through all his senses—to taste and touch, to smell and hear, to see; through sight came insight—was his perennial pursuit. There was to be no separation between him and his land. Thus his most pleasurable means of locomotion was walking, often alone, every afternoon. If we go by car we are once, twice, thrice removed, by speed, by conveyance, and by sound of motor. Moreover, we must follow their path, not our own.

Being such a consummate, wise traveler is a tall order. So keep in mind that Thoreau did not want us to be like him. No, he preferred we find our own calling and rhythm. Please, he counseled, "step to the music" you hear. Remember, too, that this is an art; like gardening, it involves planting, cultivation, weeding, practice, patience, and other virtues. Most of all, "We must learn to reawaken and keep ourselves awake," he instructed. "To affect the quality of the day, that is the highest of the arts."

While celebrating living in one place, however, Thoreau also left Concord on many occasions. He had "a penchant for paradox," as Alan D. Hodder said in *Thoreau's Ecstatic Witness*. In May 1843, he went to live on Staten Island where he tutored William Emerson's children until homesickness brought him home, after Thanksgiving. He visited Harvard's library, friends in Worcester and New Bedford, Massachusetts. He lectured in a host of towns: Philadelphia (the farthest south), Nantucket, and Portland, Maine, among them. His longest trip—two months, and the farthest west he traveled—was to Minnesota for his health, in 1861. In addition, he made three trips to Maine's interior (his farthest east was Molunkus), four to Cape Cod's eastern shore, and one Canadian excursion, from Montreal to Quebec to Mont Sainte Anne, the farthest north.

Tom Slayton inspires us to know Thoreau through the places he knew. Slayton is a reliable, sensitive, and entertaining guide. The editor emeritus of *Vermont Life*, he has a long connection with New England and Thoreau. His first reading of Thoreau—*Cape Cod*—he tells us occurred on the Cape in the 1970s in "a small cabin in South Wellfleet that sits atop the high bank overlooking the North Atlantic." This was generative. Then and there he set off to track the author in the sand and, later, in the krummholz of Katahdin. An avid climber, Slayton has attained the tops of all New England's four-thousand-footers. He was drawn naturally to Thoreau's mountains: Washington, Monadnock, Greylock, Kineo, and Katahdin, with which he exhibits a special affinity. He also paddled the Concord and the Merrimack rivers, walked about Walden Pond and Woods. In Maine, he stayed at the Chesuncook Lake House in August 2006, in the very spot of Ansel Smith's farm and lodge for lumbermen, where Thoreau had rested a night one hundred and fifty years earlier. Relaxing on the inn's porch, Slayton savored the scene: beyond the long lake at his feet the grand forest rose to Katahdin in the southeast.

While "searching for Thoreau," Slayton, a wise traveler, is aware of our relationship with nature. To see that our connection is reciprocal, to live in harmony with our precious planet, to balance our needs to converse with our surroundings and to conserve them—these are the tenets that Thoreau ardently advocated so as to keep "the New World *new*."

J. Parker Huber
Brattleboro, Vermont
12 July 2007, Thoreau's 190th Birthday

Acknowledgments

This book is deeply indebted to the work, over the past century, of Thoreau scholars, critics, and writers who have studied and puzzled over the life and activities of the complex, stubborn genius from Concord. I am especially grateful for the warm support and friendship given me in this project by J. Parker Huber, whose research on Thoreau's travels has been much deeper than my own. His generosity has been expressed on many levels, especially in his willingness to contribute a foreword to this book and his companionship on some of the hikes. I have also benefited from the scholarship of Thoreau biographer Walter Harding and from the work of William Howarth, who also deeply researched Thoreau's travels. Lawrence Buell's work on Thoreau, and the Transcendentalists generally, has helped me place Thoreau in the context of scholarly and popular opinion down through the years.

I also owe much to my friends who accompanied me on the various hikes and excursions described in these pages. Scott and Mary Skinner supplied energy and enthusiasm on many outings, and Scott on several hikes was not only friend and companion but also self-appointed chauffeur as well. Michael Katzenberg, Linda Prescott, Peter and Valerie Bluhm, John and Diane Holme, and others have shared the miles and tolerated my obsession with Thoreau and the places he visited. Jayne Gordon, director of the Thoreau Society when this book was being written, helped me better understand Thoreau's relationship with Concord and Walden Pond.

I thank my publisher, Tordis Ilg Isselhardt, for her deep faith in and enthusiasm for this project. It was a chance conversation with her four years ago that helped turn a single essay into a book. The publishing team she assembled, editor Sarah Novak and designers Ron Toelke and Barbara Kempler-Toelke, have worked diligently to improve my manuscript and transform it into a beautiful book. I am grateful to them.

Merrill Leffler, owner/publisher of Dryad Press, read and offered helpful editorial suggestions on most of the chapters.

I also must thank David and Laurie Sexton for nearly thirty years of hospitality and unforgettable ocean views at their cabin colony in South Wellfleet, Cape Cod, Cook's By The Ocean.

I am grateful to my son, Ethan, who contributed his talents as an artist to the project, and his strong back in helping me wrestle my big canoe on and off the car for the chapter on the Concord and Merrimack rivers. And my dear wife, Elizabeth, has bolstered and cheered me on, and given thoughtful criticism to the manuscript and invaluable counsel in every area of this project and my life. I could not have done it without her help.

Finally, I want to somehow, inadequately, express my thanks for the life and spirit of Henry David Thoreau. This book is, more than anything else, a monument to his passion, brilliance, and courage.

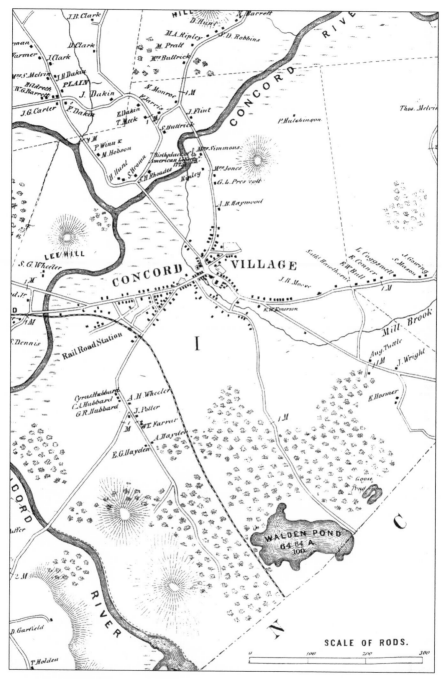

Compiled by Herbert W. Gleason, 1906

Introduction

It was September of 1857. Henry Thoreau and his friend Edward Hoar had gotten themselves completely lost, deep in the swampy forests of northern Maine. Their Indian guide, Joe Polis, had gone ahead of them, portaging their birchbark canoe to Mud Pond. He had told the two to follow his tracks, but they had taken a wrong turn and were hopelessly off course.

Henry knew they had lost the trail, but he stubbornly kept going, following his compass deeper and deeper into the chaotic recesses of a huge cedar swamp.

The going was tough. With every step, they sank into muck and water over their ankles, sometimes over their knees. Thoreau was packing about sixty pounds of gear on his back. Hoar had a similar load that he would set down while he and Thoreau broke trail, then go back and fetch forward. This tactic meant that he had to walk the entire arduous, swampy way three times.

In addition to slogging through the deep mud, the two men had to climb over scores of fallen trees, burdened further by their packs. Black-flies chewed on them mercilessly, but they battled onward. For hours.

"The fallen trees were so numerous," Thoreau wrote, "that for long distances the route was through a succession of small yards, where we climbed over fences as high as our heads, down into water often up to our knees, and then over another fence into a second yard, and so on." Except for the fallen trees, he wrote, it was so wet they could have paddled the route in a canoe.

They struggled through the first swamp, went over a small hill that gave them no view of the surrounding country at all, then descended into a second swamp. History does not record what Edward Hoar may have said or thought as Thoreau led on, following his compass bearing ever farther into the tangled morass. It is probably just as well.

At around noon their guide, Joe Polis, found them. All three agreed that the Concord men had veered well off the proper path and had completely missed Mud Pond. The Indian "evidently thought little of our woodcraft," Thoreau reported dryly.

They decided that Thoreau and Hoar should soldier on with their loads, and head directly east, aiming for Chamberlain Lake, a huge lake that would be hard for them to miss (but not impossible, obviously). Polis would retrace his steps to Mud Pond and paddle the canoe from there into Chamberlain Lake, with the aim of meeting his two charges before dark on the lake's western shore.

The two Concord men went back to picking their way laboriously through cedar swamps and over low hills. The sun began to set. After a quick conference, Thoreau went on ahead, hoping to find the lake shore before dark, leaving Hoar to beetle back and forth, ferrying his pack along on his own.

Fortunately, Polis made the west shore of Chamberlain Lake in time. He found Henry, extracted Hoar from the swamp, and the three men got to Chamberlain Lake just as the last rays of light were fading. They collapsed into the lake fully clothed to wash off the mud that covered them to the waist.

They ate a late supper and fell asleep by the shore, too exhausted to pitch their tent. Mosquitoes and tiny blackflies tortured them through the night.

Thoreau seems to have been undaunted by any of this. He botanized cheerfully as he slogged along, reported the birds and animals he encountered, and made little jokes about his predicament. His writing throughout the episode is completely good-natured, and he summarizes the experience wittily:

"If you want an exact recipe for making such a road, take one part Mud Pond, and dilute it with equal parts Umbazookskus and Apmoojenegamook; then send a family of musquash [muskrats] through to locate it, look after the grades and culverts, and finish it to their minds, and let a hurricane follow to do the fencing."

He was in high good humor, clearly delighted by his forced march.

"As it was, I would not have missed that walk for a good deal," he declared. He relates this episode in the final chapter of *The Maine Woods*, in which he details his 1857 trip to northern Maine.

Travel through the wilds made Thoreau buoyantly happy. Almost every summer of his adult life, he made it a point to get out of Concord and go to the ocean or deep into the forest. Even while in retreat at Walden Pond, in his second summer there, he left to go to northern Maine, paddle and pole his way upriver, and climb almost to the summit of Katahdin, Maine's highest mountain.

Many of his treks were what we today would call "adventure travel." What drove him to seek adventure, again and again, was his passion for wildness. He studiously avoided the fashionable vacation spots of his day, resorts like Nantasket or Newport. Instead, he went to places that most people avoided: remote mountains, the wild frontier of New England in northern Maine, or the devastated landscape of Cape Cod. He went to explore, to observe, to botanize. Sometimes his journeys left him fatigued and physically miserable. But he went anyway, because he could bear fatigue and misery. But he could not live without wildness.

He was a good Romantic, so part of what he sought was the Sublime —the sense of awestruck wonder in raging storms or vast mountain scenes that in the conventional Romanticism of his day denoted the presence of God. But he was also a naturalist, and came to understand that *wildness* did not have to be found only in *wilderness*. He wrote in his journal that true wildness was just as present in the quiet woods of Concord as it was in the deep forests of northern Maine. For him, it was a pervasive quality—close to what the ancient Chinese called the Tao, the mysterious, all-encompassing force that winds the mainspring of the universe. He searched for it everywhere.

Though his quest was serious enough, in his travel writings Thoreau was seldom in prophetic mode. He is not the angry reformer of *Walden* nor the passionate tax resister of "Civil Disobedience." He is on vacation, relaxed and witty.

However, he is still Thoreau. He doesn't hesitate to call social evils as he sees them, jabbing at windy preachers and the established church in *Cape Cod*, at the timber business in *The Maine Woods*, at his more conventional Concord neighbors in *Walden* and his journals—and, in fact, whenever he happens to feel like it.

Thoreau's major journeys were quests, pilgrimages. He treasured what he saw and learned there, and he characteristically ended each foray into the wilderness by returning to Concord, reconciled, seeing anew the goodness of his town and his neighbors.

"Nevertheless, it was a relief to get back to our smooth, but still varied landscape," he writes near the end of "Chesuncook," the second chapter in *The Maine Woods*, describing his return to Concord after his 1853 trip to northern Maine. "For a permanent residence, it seemed to me that there could be no comparison between this and the wilderness, necessary as the latter is for a resource and background, the raw material of all our civilization."

That he loved wildness yet rejoiced when he returned to civilization is but one of the many contradictions in Thoreau's life. He was the nature lover who started forest fires, the hermit who went regularly to the post office and lived most of his life with his parents, the stern reformer with a puckish sense of humor who could play exuberantly, loved children, and gave what his neighbors regarded as the best melon parties in Concord.

Yet he was consistent throughout his life in his love of walking, in writing and keeping his journal, and in his ever-deepening botanical study. He was also consistent in his affection for particular places. The titles of his most familiar books name some of them: *Walden, Cape Cod, The Maine Woods*. What he found there changed him and helped him develop as a person and as a writer.

Walden Pond was undoubtedly the most important of all his places. His two-year retreat there gave him the time and quiet he needed to recover from the death of his elder brother, John. He wrote most of his first book, *A Week on the Concord and Merrimack Rivers*, at the pond, and dedicated it to John's memory. It was also there that he confirmed his vocation as a writer and began the masterpiece that he would later entitle *Walden*.

He wrote up his earliest mountain climbs as intellectual, Romantic journeys, filled with classical references and appropriate thoughts. But gradually, as he gained years and experience, his writing deepened. His later essays were studded with fewer classical references (though he never really gave up the habit), and they contained more—much more— acute factual observation.

Part of his development may have come from an important experience he had in 1846, on the stony heights of Katahdin. While climbing that mountain, Thoreau's evolution as a naturalist took a crucial turn when he encountered a face of nature he had not known before. It was stern, stark, and forbidding, and it shook him to his core.

Although he never climbed on Katahdin again, he took two more trips to northern Maine, one of them a major expedition in which he traveled on both the West and East Branches of the Penobscot and traveled through an immense swath of the wildest country in New England, completely circumnavigating the peak. He was rained on a lot during both of those trips, had a couple of good scares, and had his preconceptions—especially his Romantic ideas about Native Americans— rearranged many times. Yet his account of each adventure is filled with wonder and often, incongruously, with good humor and wit.

His several trips to Cape Cod also helped temper and develop his writing. There Thoreau found the existential wildness he loved woven into a devastated landscape inhabited by tough, resilient New Englanders who worked on and coped with the wild North Atlantic every day of their lives. In their fishing trips out onto the storm-ridden ocean, the unrelenting labor of their lives, even the stunted gardens and shrunken apple trees they tended in the Cape's eroding sands, Thoreau saw different aspects of a life he admired. It was a hard life, based in a stern reality. Yet the people of the Cape bore it without complaint, and often enriched it with humor and hope. Ironically, the raging sea and wrecked landscape of the Cape inspired some of his most playful and humorous prose.

Thoreau's writings about place are maps of his personal development. They are also maps, plain and simple: they tell us where he went and what he saw. Because he wrote so precisely about his travels, his books and essays lend themselves to rediscovery. You can trace his footsteps from the evidence they present. It is clear, for example, that in his epic climb up Katahdin he got to the top of the jumbled rock ridge connecting Baxter and South peaks, but never made the summit. The Outer Beach at Cape Cod Thoreau walked can still be walked today; many of his landmarks still exist. And scholars have made careers out of identifying and naming the points around Concord that he visited. The best evidence of all this and more can be found in his writings.

Searching for Thoreau is an attempt to encounter and understand Henry David Thoreau through place—the specific places in New England that he journeyed to and wrote about. It is not a biography of Thoreau, still less a scholarly study of his travel writings or of *Walden*. It is simply my attempt to connect with Thoreau and to understand him better by visiting the places that were most important to him. For the past few years I have been going to those places with Thoreau in mind, and writing about them, and him. They were almost all in New England, and so my search focused there.

I have enjoyed the project enormously. Not only did I visit some of the most beautiful and interesting spots in New England, I also got to see them through the eyes of a fascinating, very quirky writer. Reading Thoreau deeply is a little like riding a mountain bike down a twisting mountain trail: you don't know whether you're in for a long, gradual runout, an unannounced right-angle turn, or a blind jump that will catapult you into thin air. He doesn't always go where you expect him to.

But in searching for Thoreau's New England, I found Thoreau as well. Reading him repeatedly and going to the places he wrote about helped me know him better. I learned a deeper admiration for his accomplishments as a man and as a writer. Even into early middle age he remained physically and mentally tough, able to walk and paddle long distances, idealistic, sharply observant, as well as resilient and witty in adversity.

My personal journey with this brilliant, troublesome, contradictory, undeniably great writer actually began some thirty years earlier. It was in the early 1970s, on my first trip to Cape Cod, when I bought and read the book of the same name. I was immediately taken by its dry, humorous tone and the fact that I could so obviously see before me the actual Cape Thoreau was writing about.

My wife Elizabeth and I had rented a small cabin in South Wellfleet that sits atop the high bank overlooking the North Atlantic. (We have been going there almost every summer since.) We could see the beach and the ocean; I could feel the wind and hear the surf booming as I read the passage in which Thoreau describes the Outer Beach for the first time:

"There I had got the Cape under me, as much as if I were riding it bare-backed. It was not as on the map, or seen from the stage-coach; but there I found it all out-of-doors, huge and real, Cape Cod!"

Well, yes! After reading that, I wanted to join Thoreau on the Outer Beach, and shortly afterwards, I did, taking a day-long journey, twenty miles along the Outer Beach between Wellfleet and Race Point, near Provincetown. It was the first of many long walks on the Cape, some of them following Thoreau, some following my own inclination. Over many summers, my wife, Elizabeth, son, Ethan, and I got to know the Outer Cape well. I soaked up information about it like a sponge, learned to go when the overpowering summertime crowds were absent, and worried as I watched development consume more and more of the unprotected places there.

About the same time, I made my first trip to Katahdin. I have returned there many times also, and have happily absorbed its sheer rocky grandeur and its palpable feeling of wildness. It is, as its Penobscot name suggests, New England's greatest mountain.

More recently I have been filling in the blank spaces on my map of Thoreau's New England. From the quiet trails of woodland Concord and the shores of Walden Pond, to the far reaches of northern Maine, I've spent years now, trying to catch up to him. And I have found echoes of Thoreau, resonances of Thoreau in many of those places. Some were subtle, like the delicate three-toothed cinquefoil and blue harebells blossoming on Mount Kineo in northern Maine, likely the descendants of the cinquefoil and harebells Thoreau himself saw there. Others were more obvious, like the rocks inscribed with quotations from Thoreau's journal that I nearly stumbled over alongside the paved paths atop Mount Greylock in western Massachusetts.

Not surprisingly, I also found that many parts of Thoreau's New England have been compromised.

The woods of northern Maine have been savagely logged. Much of Cape Cod that lay in waste in Thoreau's time is now overdeveloped and, in the summer months, swamped with tourists. While the summit of Katahdin remains undeveloped and wild, the top of New England's highest peak, Mount Washington (which Thoreau also climbed) is virtually blanketed with parking lots, railroad tracks and platforms, communications towers, and a sprawling concrete summit building.

The relentless imperatives of our modern consumer economy— including the recreation economy—have trampled a lot of wild New England. However, a surprising amount of that New England remains. It can be seen and visited. And it can help us understand the breadth of Thoreau's experience as a naturalist and environmental advocate—and the depth of his achievement as a writer.

Perhaps by learning to appreciate the wild lands of New England that remain, we will also strengthen our determination to protect them. That would surely please even the hard-to-please Mr. Thoreau.

Not a fish can leap or an insect fall on the pond but it is thus reported in circling dimples, in lines of beauty, as it were the constant welling up of its fountain, the gentle pulsing of its life, the heaving of its breast. . . . How peaceful the phenomena of the lake! Again the works of man shine as in the spring. Ay, every leaf and twig and stone and cobweb sparkles now at mid-afternoon as when covered with dew in a spring morning. Every motion of an oar or an insect produces a flash of light; and if an oar falls, how sweet the echo!

—Walden

1

Walden Pond and *Walden*

The spot where Henry David Thoreau spent two years living in the woods beside Walden Pond has become a small, unofficial shrine, complete with interpretative signs and a cairn.

In late fall, the glen where his tiny cabin stood is carpeted with brown leaves; the November trees are bare and open to the autumn sky. To the south, through the tall oaks and pines, you can see the shining surface of the pond and the wooded hills above the opposite shore. A leaf-covered woods road—little more than a path, actually—leads up from the water, and I wonder, idly, as I climb it, how often Thoreau might have walked the same path.

The place where his cabin stood on a gently sloping shelf above the lake is marked by granite posts. Like any proper New Englander, I find a stone and add it to the cairn nearby.

The pond is clear and sandy-bottomed today, just as it was in Thoreau's day. There's a small, sheltered embayment, now appropriately called "Thoreau's Cove," just down from the cabin, most likely the spot where he swam in the pond each morning. I can see that autumn's fallen leaves have drifted into the cove and make a colored mosaic on its ribbed sandy bottom, an effect that Thoreau had written about a century and a half before.

Though the woods and the cove are pretty, Walden Pond today is neither secluded nor especially picturesque. It is a state park now, and is crowded in the summer. A public beach at the pond's east end attracts hundreds of swimmers every day, and the pond's parking lots fill up early.

The most direct route to the actual site of Thoreau's cabin is not a pristine stroll. A determined bankside conservation project has fenced in both sides of the shoreline path, so one walks alongside the pond hemmed in by wire fences.

At the cove, a half-mile from the beach, the parking lot, and the inevitable gift shop, brightly clad joggers occasionally trot by, chatting. Through the trees, busy Route 2 can be heard, a constant river of red taillights rushing into Boston.

Yet if there is sacred ground in New England, it is here. For here is where *Walden*, one of the great classics of American literature, was conceived and partly written. Here is where Thoreau declared his independence from the way American society was going (and goes ever more rapidly today). Here is one of the brood sites for New England individualism and New England environmentalism.

And here also, to be honest, is the birthplace of a truly *strange* great book.

In 2004, it had been 150 years since *Walden* was first published, and there were at least three special "150th Anniversary Editions" just out. And so I read the book again, just to see what I might find there. I had studied it in college and reread parts of it down through the years but, somehow, *Walden*'s profound oddness never before impressed itself on me.

Others have noticed it. Poet and critic Hayden Carruth even went so far, in a poem, to refer to "that idiot, Thoreau," and, in a subsequent slashing essay, to castigate the great naturalist soundly for the disdain and scorn with which Thoreau writes about his Concord neighbors.

"It is an elitist manifesto," wrote Carruth, "a cranky, crabby diatribe."

One could accuse Carruth of being a bit crabby himself. But he has a point. Parts of *Walden* are undeniably grumpy and preachy—but only parts. Especially in its first two chapters, Thoreau does a lot of angry complaining about the evils of society in general and his neighbors in particular. Much of his first chapter, "Economy," is judgmental and distasteful in tone.

"It is very evident what mean and sneaking lives many of you live," he writes sourly, "lying, flattering, voting, contracting yourself into a nutshell of civility or dilating into an atmosphere of thin and vaporous generosity. . . ."

Most men, he declares, "lead lives of quiet desperation."

"From the desperate city you go into the desperate country, and have to console yourself with the bravery of minks and muskrats."

This is great invective, grand social criticism, and, frankly, Thoreau is right most of the time. But after a while, it becomes tiring. Thoreau continues for pages and pages in this manner, cutting away at everyone (it seems) but himself for cowardice, subservience, and conformity. His other equally unpleasant tactic in "Economy" is to praise his own independence and to justify his own experience and habits. At one point, he even pats himself on the back for getting up earlier in the morning than his Concord neighbors.

"How many mornings, summer and winter, before yet any neighbor was stirring about his business, have I been about mine!" he writes, adding a pompous exclamation point.

There is humor in *Walden*, but in the book's first two chapters, "Economy" and "Where I Lived and What I Lived For," it is often sarcastic, cutting, and self-justifying, the sort of humor that scores points and keeps track of them.

If Thoreau had written only those first two chapters, in which he lays out his reasons for going off to the pond to live, and bashes the rest of Concord for not doing the same, *Walden* probably would never have attained its international status as a Great Book. Most likely it would have been cast aside as the grumpy mutterings of the village malcontent.

That, in fact, is how Henry David Thoreau was viewed by many in Concord—not only in 1845 when he went to Walden Pond, but also for most of his life. Bright and Harvard-educated, he had by 1845 failed at just about everything he had tried: school teaching, odd jobs, freelance writing. Eventually he was able to make a modest living as a surveyor.

For many of the Concord bourgeoisie, Thoreau was the perfect example of the educated fool. Just two years before, he and a fishing companion had accidentally sparked a disastrous forest fire and burned three hundred acres of valuable woods. Many people remembered him ever after not as a writer or surveyor, but as "the man who burned the forest."

The one woman he seriously courted, the beautiful Ellen Sewall, had already turned him down. And the death of his brother, John, in 1842 had plunged him into a lengthy depression so severe that his friend Ralph Waldo Emerson had urged him to follow his heart and build a solitary cabin by the shores of Walden Pond. Emerson owned a plot of land there, which he let Henry build upon, and Thoreau refers to himself in Walden as a "squatter"—the contemporary term for one who lived without title on someone else's property.

So it's fairly easy to see why, by the time he built his cabin, Thoreau, a stubborn, self-righteous man by nature, was primed to churn out a bilious diatribe angrily, defensively justifying himself, his motives, his genius, and his own personal vision of the world as it should be.

Thoreau's scorn for the world of everyday commerce echoes through the smoldering early chapters of *Walden*. Part of that is knee-jerk sour grapes, but Thoreau is also writing as a determined reformer. He was well aware of the utopian ideals of Brook Farm, one of the great, hopelessly idealistic social experiments of the 19th century. Established in nearby West Roxbury, Brook Farm was the ultimate in 19th-century political correctness. It was a high-minded commune, a conscious attempt to create a simpler, more wholesome society of liberal, cultivated people unstained by commerce.

Thoreau wanted nothing to do with communal living, but he shared much of the era's intellectual distaste for emerging 19th-century commercialism. In moving from busy Concord village (where he lived with his parents) to the wooded shores of the pond, Thoreau thought of himself as a New Social Order of one, a kind of one-person Brook Farm.

His reformist instinct is commendable: any thoughtful observer knows that American society is chronically unfair and materialistic. It badly needs improvement. But Thoreau's tone is often savage. Even when he selects a plump, juicy target, he often drifts into outrage and hyperbole and demolishes it so viciously that the reader winces and wonders what is ailing him.

And he all too often forgets his own shortcomings, the number of free dinners he had at home and at Emerson's—and the fact that he was living rent-free on Emerson's land:

"To maintain one's self on this earth is not a hardship but a pastime, if we will live simply and wisely," he declares. "It is not necessary that a man should earn his living by the sweat of his brow, unless he sweats easier than I do."

This is both glib and arrogant, and ultimately seems a bit of a pose, as do other passages of self-justification and social reform found early in his book.

— — —

But there is another Henry David Thoreau living in the pages of *Walden*, a witty, elegant writer with a clear eye and something important to say, a man with reserves of intelligence, humor, even self-knowledge.

This is the Thoreau who describes briskly and accurately how he built his house and how much it cost, who looks at nature closely and finds worlds to describe in an anthill or a loon or a thawing sandy bank. This is the Thoreau who made the first complete survey of Walden Pond and wrote eloquently of its beauty in all seasons. Ultimately, he compressed two years' worth of living by the pond into a single seasonal round and came to know the natural world intimately, and himself as a part of it.

This is the Thoreau who writes about the deep question that motivated him:

"I went to the woods because I wished to live deliberately, to front only the essential facts of life, and see if I could not learn what it had to teach, and not, when I came to die, discover that I had not lived."

Thoreau ultimately found what he was looking for. Life responded, and its response is in his book. *Walden* is the record, both external and internal, of how he discovered what life had to teach him.

Somehow during the two years he lived alongside the pond, Thoreau progressed beyond mere ranting and posturing; he grew there and matured as a writer and a human being. The pages of *Walden* document that growth, which is one of the reasons it is a great book, and why it must be read as a whole to be fully appreciated. Though grounded in place most specifically, Thoreau's book describes—among many other things—a profound journey that the failed schoolteacher, writer, handyman, and lover took within himself.

Some of Thoreau's best writing in *Walden* comes when he forgets all his theories and focuses on specifics: what he saw and what he did. Then his writing becomes clear and forceful, the sarcasm and rhetorical devices drop away, and we can hear an attractive voice telling us something we long to hear.

We see glimpses of Thoreau's better side in *Walden*'s first chapters; more of it emerges later in the book. The tone of his writing changes. He becomes less acerbic, less self-important. The eminent Harvard scholar and authority on the Transcendentalist writers, Lawrence Buell, in a brilliant analysis of Thoreau's nature writing, points out that Thoreau's "favorite pronoun"—"I"—appears 6.6 times per page in the first two chapters of *Walden*, and decreases in frequency throughout the book. In Walden's final five chapters, it appears 3.6 times per page.

And so, *Walden* lightens up as it goes along. Thoreau becomes a better companion, less crabby and more entertaining. He gives us beautiful passages in which he observes nature closely and writes about his observations with clarity and restraint. He employs humor more frequently. And, wonder of wonders, he comes to accept, even (sometimes) to feel affection for his fellow townspeople. These passages gradually become more and more the fabric of the book.

In one famous bravura passage on the railroad that skirted the west end of Walden Pond, Thoreau suggests that the railroad runs on the bodies of the men who built it and declares that he won't have his ears "spoiled" by its noise. But when he simply listens to the rush of the train it becomes just another sound to him and he can comment on it wittily, noting that the steam plume from the train is "going to heaven while the cars are going to Boston," and a few pages later he even says that he likes the "enterprise and bravery" of commerce, adding "it is very natural in its methods."

The same Thoreau who earlier condemned everyone else in town for their cowardice and desperation now hears the Sunday church bells as "a faint, sweet, and, as it were, natural melody, worth importing into the wilderness." His anger at Concord society seems to be abating.

What is it that brings about this gradual change in him? The process of rewriting may have helped. Thoreau rewrote *Walden* seven times over the years between 1845 and 1853. But there is another, deeper reason also. My own feeling is that solitude and silence in a beautiful natural setting—the simple, inescapable regimen of time spent alone beside Walden Pond—helped Thoreau heal and mature as a writer.

He tells us as much in the fourth chapter of *Walden*, "Sounds."

"I did not read books the first summer; I hoed beans," he writes and then confesses that sometimes he did something even better: that is, he did nothing.

"Sometimes, in a summer morning, having taken my accustomed bath, I sat in my sunny doorway from sunrise till noon, rapt in a revery, amidst the pines and the hickories and sumachs, in undisturbed solitude and stillness, while the birds sang around or flitted noiseless through the house. . . ."

"I grew in those seasons," he tells us, "like corn in the night, and they were far better than any work of the hands would have been."

This was Thoreau's seed-time, a season of contemplative growth when he somehow assimilated the failures of his past, healed from the loss of his brother, and clarified his vision, all by simply sitting in the sunlight, wrapped in the calm beauty of the natural world. It wasn't formal meditation. But anyone who has spent time outdoors, absorbing nature's beauty, would understand the process.

It is precisely at this point that *Walden*'s balance shifts and Thoreau begins to seem more approachable, less odd. His writing generally becomes less puffy and self-righteous.We get more genius and less rant the farther we get into the book.

However, Thoreau is still Thoreau and there are many strange side jaunts as Walden progresses, some effective and others less so. He's a very circuitous writer, and the texture of the book is uneven. Partially, this was intentional. In structuring *Walden*, Thoreau arranged his chapters in pairs that complement and contrast with one another. For example, his chapter on "Solitude" is followed by one on "Visitors," and the wonderful chapter on "Sounds" is preceded by a considerably less wonderful chapter on "Reading," an exhortation to read the classics and avoid novels and newspapers.

There's a clue to another reason for the packed, choppy quality of *Walden* quite early in the book. Thoreau, nattering on about the triviality of most business and daily affairs, declares that he could get along perfectly well without the post office:

"I never received more than one or two letters in my life—I wrote this some years ago—that were worth the postage."

(One of his acquaintances later noted that few people were more faithful in their visits to the Concord post office than Henry Thoreau.)

At any rate, Thoreau notes that he wrote the passage "some years ago" in his masterwork, his multi-volumed journal. In fact, much of *Walden* is mined from that journal—cut, pasted, and edited to fit—which accounts for the bumpy, too-full quality of some sections of the book.

— — —

Thoreau possessed many practical skills that other Concord Transcendentalists lacked. He was handy with tools, became an accomplished surveyor and builder, and learned enough masonry to build a working chimney and fireplace to heat his cabin. He had helped his father build a house in Concord the year before, so the Walden cabin was not a daunting project.

He notes that he installed a stove for his second winter "since I did not own the forest."

However, his attempts at both science and economics, as expressed in *Walden*, are generally fanciful, at best. After accurately surveying, sounding, and mapping Walden Pond, he quickly disposes of the local notion that it is bottomless. Historically, Thoreau's is the first complete and accurate survey of the pond.

But then, noting that the greatest depth of the pond (107 feet) occurs at the intersection of lines drawn through its greatest length and breadth, he goes on to suggest this as an absolute geographic law, governing the depth of all bodies of water, including the oceans!

Having established his "law" he proceeds to extend it, playfully, to human personality. Where the lines drawn through a man's behavior and habits intersect, he proposes, "will be the height or depth of his character."

It may be a witty, imaginative truth, but it is obviously a long way from a scientific one.

What Thoreau did most of at Walden Pond was write—more and better than he had ever done before. During his two years beside the pond, he wrote most of *A Week on the Concord and Merrimack Rivers* and *Walden*, the only two books he wrote that were published during his lifetime. He also maintained his journals and worked extensively on other essays. More importantly, his writing improved, vastly. His retreat to the pond was less an economic experiment (as he presented it) than a writer's retreat. It gave him time to contemplate and mature.

John Updike notes, in his introduction to the Princeton University Press edition of *Walden*, that Thoreau went to his pondside cabin an unknown youth of twenty-seven, and returned to Concord two years later "as essentially the Thoreau known to literary history."

In the middle chapters of the book—"The Bean-Field," "The Village," "The Ponds," and "Baker Farm"—he explores Walden, Concord, the lands around, and his life therein. He hoes his beans, visits other inhabitants of the woods, and watches nature.

His observations ring with honesty and directness. When a wood-chuck crosses his path, he confesses that he has a sudden impulse to seize the creature and devour it raw—an urge possibly explained by the fact that he was living mainly on a vegetarian diet of cornmeal, rice, and molasses at the time! Thoreau comments in another place that he did eat a woodchuck that was ravaging his bean field, and that he found it musky, but quite tasty otherwise. He also recommends vegetarianism—such are the happy contradictions of his experiment in simple living.

As noted earlier, his feelings toward the village grew more temperate, even affectionate, and, by the middle of the book, he could even poke a little fun at himself. Noting that while building his fireplace chimney, he slept on the floor for a while with some bricks for a pillow, he adds, "Yet I did not get a stiff neck for it that I remember; my stiff neck is of older date."

His writing becomes subtler and more graceful also. In the same chapter ("House-Warming"), he effortlessly drops one of his loveliest metaphors when he notes that in the last warm days of November he liked to sun himself sitting on Walden's northeastern shore, which he referred to as "the fire-side of the pond":

"I thus warmed myself by the still glowing embers which the summer, like a departed hunter, had left."

Walden gradually moves into a description of the seasonal cycle and there are many encounters with nature that are deep and beautiful. Nature closely observed becomes his forte as the book progresses. He displays an easy familiarity with the woods, the ponds, and his animal neighbors that is unsentimental, unromantic, yet thoroughly charming.

The mystery and beauty of nature begin to impress him. In his most lyrical chapter, "The Ponds," he sees Walden Pond as pure, austere, and reserved, yet also mysterious, possessed of spiritual power. In one of several lovely, dreamlike passages, he writes of watching the "trembling circles" that appear on Walden's surface on completely calm days:

"Not a fish can leap or an insect fall on the pond but it is thus reported in circling dimples, in lines of beauty, as it were the constant welling up

of its fountain, the gentle pulsing of its life, the heaving of its breast. . . .
How peaceful the phenomena of the lake! Again the works of man shine
as in the spring. Ay, every leaf and twig and stone and cobweb sparkles
now at mid-afternoon as when covered with dew in a spring morning.
Every motion of an oar or an insect produces a flash of light; and if an
oar falls, how sweet the echo!"

Even the humblest, most common creatures are seen as vital connec-
tions in the web of nature, and fascinating in their own right. There is
the famous battle of red and black ants, of course, that every schoolchild
has read, a set piece of careful reporting. *Walden* also contains many crisp,
evocative descriptions of animals—foxes, loons, mice, hares, and a memorable barred owl that the naturalist discovered on one of his winter walks.

The owl hears Thoreau but can't see him and after a while half-closes
his eyes and begins to nod. Thoreau also begins to feel sleepy watching the owl, who keeps watching him sleepily back. Finally "spreading
his wings to unexpected breadth" the bird flies silently off through the
snowy pines:

"Thus, guided amid the pine boughs rather by a delicate sense of
their neighborhood than by sight, feeling his twilight way as it were with
his sensitive pinions, he found a new perch, where he might in peace
await the dawning of his day."

Such experiences were deeply valuable to Thoreau. As spring—and
the conclusion of his book—approaches, the tone of his writing increases
in passion and he fires off volleys of thoughts, images, and metaphors.

The frost comes out of the ground, he says, "like a dormant quadruped
from its burrow, and seeks the sea with music, or migrates to other climes
in clouds." The entire earth is "living poetry, like the leaves of a tree."

A handmade, self-discovered kind of New England Taoism emerges
from *Walden* that owes as much to Thoreau's own powers of thought and
observation as to his voluminous readings in Eastern literature. He sees
humanity, at its simplest and most honest, as part of the natural world, and
Concord itself as spiritually dependent upon the wildlands around it:

"Our village life would stagnate if it were not for the unexplored forests and meadows which surround it," he writes. "We need the tonic of wildness,—to wade sometimes in marshes where the bittern and mead-ow-hen lurk, and hear the booming of the snipe; to smell the whispering sedge where only some wilder and more solitary fowl builds her nest, and the mink crawls with its belly close to the ground. . . . We need to witness our own limits transgressed and some life pasturing freely where we never wander."

This is more than Romantic veneration of nature and more than Transcendental identification of human and natural worlds; it suggests that the life-force expressed in nature actually drives the village and its human inhabitants as well as the life of field and forest. For Thoreau it has become all one thing: the railroad, the loons, the woods, his friend the wood-chopper Alek Therrien, the field mice, the village, the marshes, and the ponds. Bitterness at past failure has no place there, nor does resentment, with its focus on the past:

"We should be blessed if we lived in the present always," he writes. "We loiter in winter while it is already spring. . . . Through our own recovered innocence we discern the innocence of our neighbors."

This insight leads Thoreau, in his "Conclusion," to an understanding of what he has seen and accomplished. His last chapter is the answer to his first, both in style and content, and, though he returns to his role as social reformer, he subtly includes himself among those requiring reform.

He did learn something while at the pond, Thoreau tells us, and it wasn't about economics or science:

"I learned this, at least, by my experiment; that if one advances con-fidently in the direction of his dreams, and endeavors to live the life which he has imagined, he will meet with a success unexpected in com-mon hours. . . . In proportion as he simplifies his life, the laws of the universe will appear less complex, and solitude will not be solitude, nor poverty poverty, nor weakness weakness. If you have built castles in the air, your work need not be lost; that is where they should be. Now put the foundations under them."

Finally, Thoreau declares his discovery: that we all have the capability of awakening to life and finding it miraculous. That is what has happened to him. He has been reborn.

In a metaphor of rebirth, he tells the story of the "strong and beautiful bug" that slumbered for years in a dry apple-wood table, but finally hatched and gnawed its way out.

"Who knows what beautiful and winged life, whose egg has been buried for ages under many concentric layers of woodenness in the dead dry life of society . . . may unexpectedly come forth from amidst society's most trivial and handselled furniture, to enjoy its perfect summer life at last!"

Thus Thoreau's acrid view of a flawed world has become a positive vision of self-emancipation and hope.

"There is more day to dawn," he concludes. "The sun is but a morning star."

— — —

It is still early morning as I walk back from the cabin site, toward the Walden Pond parking lot. I shuffle through leaves along a small ridge top and pick up a faint rustling that at first I take to be wind in the treetops.

But I quickly realize it is November and the trees are mostly bare. The rustling continues to grow louder. Soon it is a roar, and I half-expect to see a flight of jets come over the hills across the quiet pond.

Then I remember: it's the train! It would, in Thoreau's day, have been even louder, a steam engine hissing and roaring and belching coal smoke. It dashes across the west end of the pond and is gone, another link with the quirky genius who came here to contemplate and heal and confront his life.

As I reach the beach and the end of the woods, a red-tailed hawk calls harshly several times from somewhere almost directly above me. I watch gratefully as it soars over the pond, wild and free, then turns and disappears over the ridge to the north.

Our village life would stagnate if it were not for the unexplored forests and meadows which surround it. We need the tonic of wildness,—to wade sometimes in marshes where the bittern and the meadow-hen lurk, and hear the booming of the snipe; to smell the whispering sedge where only some wilder and more solitary fowl builds her nest, and the mink crawls with its belly close to the ground.

—Walden

2

A Walk in the Concord Woods

Near Walden Pond, nine AM on a misty Saturday in May, the skies clearing after heavy rain.

I'm here for a walk through Thoreau's woods. But we start our day of walking at Walden Pond's carefully monitored parking lots, where cars begin to pile in before nine AM and a replica of Thoreau's cabin has been constructed.

Jayne Gordon, at the time of this walk executive director of the Thoreau Society and a pleasant, round-faced woman with curly black hair, is helping a group of us shed some of our illusions about this place. She will be leading our walk to places in Concord familiar to Thoreau, such as Fair Haven Bay, Bear Garden Hill, and the Androm-eda Ponds—places that he walked to daily and then wrote about often, repeatedly, perhaps compulsively.

Jayne, who grew up in nearby Lexington, is bright and articulate, a good leader. She knows these woods intimately, having walked in them in all seasons, for most of her life. From the 1990s until 2003, she helped rock musician Don Henley raise the money needed to save them from development. Her first boyfriend, she tells us, courted her by discuss-ing philosophy as they floated in a boat on Walden Pond. But she's no Romantic. She wants us to understand the complex reality of Thoreau's world. And our own.

Those two worlds are intermingled here. An oriole sings in a nearby tree as the day's first cars begin to roll in.

There's a statue of Henry David himself out front of the replica of his cabin—three-quarter size, so he looks about as big as a twelve-year-old boy. The sculptor has depicted him in a moment of disheveled frenzy, staring intently at his hand, which he holds, fingers spread, directly in front of his face.

"Contact! Contact!" he could be saying. "Who are we? Where are we?"

Except that was his reaction to the deep Maine woods, not the parking lots of Walden Pond.

The interior of the replica hut, like the original, is ten feet wide by fifteen feet long—about the size of a small bedroom. It feels neat and spartan, not cramped. There's a narrow bed, a desk, an iron stove set in a brick fireplace, and some chairs. We look around admiringly: this wouldn't be bad at all.

Although it is an exact replica, there are a couple of obvious changes from Thoreau's own cabin. There's a lock on the door, for one thing. And a guest book, which offers visitors the chance to comment on the cabin or Thoreau or the day, or anything else. Anything else wins, hands down. "Inner peace!" one has written. Another entry declares: "Rama! Rama!" and "Rama!" with the name signed only as "Rama!"

Jayne points out the cabin's three chairs: "Thoreau said he had one chair for solitude, two for company, three for society," she says to polite laughter. Thoreau the wit, the lifelong minter of epigrams, knew quite well that his time by Walden Pond was not solitary. He often had company, sometimes more than he wanted. His comment on the chairs was probably also a subtle suggestion about the maximum size of the "society" he would appreciate having: three.

We cross the road, walk down an inclined path, and bypass the public beach, instead angling uphill into the woods. This enables us to avoid the metal fencing that lines the shoreline path and keeps people from scrambling up Walden's easily eroded, sandy banks. There are a half-dozen of us on this walk, which was organized by the Thoreau Society. I am the only male. The women are middle-aged nature fanciers. None of us is a Thoreau scholar. As we walk along a trail that climbs the little hills above the pond, Ginger Lang, proprietor of a company called Ginger's Journeys, which organizes walks in Concord and elsewhere, points out various May wildflowers—pussytoes, Carolina pinks, anemones. There are tiny white starflowers everywhere on the forest floor.

We thread our way along a ridgetop, then drop down into a little amphitheater-like bowl where there are some stumps for us to sit on. Walden Pond gleams transcendentally behind us in the morning sunlight.

"This was a very active area commercially in Thoreau's day," Jayne says. "We like to think of it as a virgin forest, but it wasn't."

By the 1840s Walden Pond was a patchwork of woodlots and timber operations. Like the rest of New England, Concord was busily cutting down its forests and burning them to heat its homes and fuel the ever-hungry railroad. Thoreau complained about the devastation of the woods in his journal, and put some of those angry passages into *Walden* and his essays. In "Life Without Principle," he wrote:

"If a man walk in the woods for love of them half of each day, he is in danger of being regarded as a loafer; but if he spends his whole day as a speculator, shearing off those woods and making the earth bald before her time, he is esteemed an industrious and enterprising citizen. As if a town had no interest in its forests but to cut them down!"

Even so, Thoreau was well aware that his occupation as a surveyor often helped enable the very cutting he lamented. "This winter they are cutting down our woods more seriously than ever," he wrote in 1852. "Fair Haven Hill—Walden . . . thank God they cannot cut down the clouds." Yet he could also convince himself that the cutting was not all bad, since it opened new views—"prospects"—for him in his walks, and he solaced himself with the belief that Walden would remain pure, even if its shores were laid bare.

The woods surrounding the pond were also where many of the town's poorest—mainly blacks, French, and Irish immigrants—lived in small shanties.

A complex time then—and today. Later in the 19th century the Emerson family came to own the pond and most of the surrounding land, which they and others subsequently gave to the county. And so it became a state park. The rights of fishermen and swimmers were specified in the will (Emerson, like Thoreau and the other Transcendentalists, swam in the pond regularly). Add to that guarantee the fact that Walden—undeniably a beautiful pond—is the nearest large body of water to Boston, and the crowds at the public beach on its east end are easy to understand. On hot summer days, the beach is jammed to overflowing; the adjacent parking lots usually are filled to capacity by nine AM.

As we walk on the hills above them, joggers have begun to pad along the paths that encircle the shoreline. At the beach, swimmers are pulling on wetsuits and getting ready to brave the chilly May waters. Amateur botanists and bird watchers—like us—are wandering the paths also.

"It's not an easy job that the park service has, to balance the various uses," Jayne notes.

We mosey along to the site of the Thoreau cabin and the memorial cairn begun by Bronson Alcott in June of 1872. The pond is visible through the trees, and I think of Henry David, out in his skiff, playing his flute to a school of perch:

"In warm evenings I frequently sat in the boat playing the flute, and saw the perch, which I seemed to have charmed, hovering around me, and the moon travelling over the ribbed bottom, which was strewed with the wrecks of the forest."

It is one of his most beautiful images, yet not without a bit of unintentional irony: the "wrecks of the forest" are relic logs from earlier timbering operations. Thoreau is serenading the perch—and waterlogged timber waste. Like us, he took his beauty where he found it.

He originally wrote the little vignette in his journal in May, 1841, four years before he actually lived at the pond. He later rewrote the passage, and shoehorned it into *Walden* as he revised it. There were to be seven complete revisions before the book was finally published in 1854.

I watch yellow-rumped warblers skimming through the May woods, and there are a few pink ladyslippers, nearly gone by, blooming not far away. We move along a well-tramped path westward through the oaks and pines to Ice Fort Cove. Thoreau named it after seeing a huge pile of cut ice blocks stacked there by Irish workmen and deciding it looked like "a vast blue fort or Valhalla." The pile was thirty-five feet high and six or seven rods square.

The ice was being cut by order of Frederic Tudor, "The Ice King of New England," Jayne tells us. Before electric refrigeration came along and changed things, Tudor made a vast fortune cutting and selling ice to fill the iceboxes of the world. His estate on Nahant Island, north of Boston, is now the Nahant Country Club, and it specializes in a more contemporary New England growth industry: weddings.

The cove is right next to the rail line, which would have been convenient for transporting the ice to Boston. From there it could be shipped around the world.

It was not a quiet cove then, and it is not quiet today: as we arrive, a small flotilla of canoes filled with kids—campers and their counselors, most likely—is paddling in to shore. They disembark efficiently, and carry their yellow and red canoes up the path, disappearing so quickly they might be a band of bright-colored little ghosts.

We clamber up a different path and cross the railroad tracks that were Thoreau's shortcut into town. Just around the bend from us is the "deep cut" where he saw sand oozing out of a thawing bank, flowing into leaflike, fractal patterns in the early spring. He wrote a lengthy, playful passage, describing the sand-flow, pushing the trope to its limits (as he was wont to do), declaring: "Thus it seemed that this one hillside illustrated the principle of all the operations of Nature. The Maker of this earth but patented a leaf."

We cross the tracks and walk through a pretty oak woods, past signs put up by the Concord Conservation Land Trust (CCLT), which has protected many acres of these woods from development. We wind our way around Bear Garden Hill, and as we near its crest the forest suddenly changes. It becomes much more open, with fewer trees, and blueberry bushes everywhere. A significant fire swept through here a few years back, opening up the woods and allowing the blueberries to flourish. My guess is that they have flourished before, and may be the reason for the hill's name—"bear garden"—since bears like blueberries.

After the fire, Jayne tells us, the hillside smelled like burnt cinnamon toast. Now, on a sunny August day, she says, "It smells like hot blueberry pie."

We are at the epicenter of the fight that took place in the late 1980s and 1990s to save Walden Woods. A developer had purchased Bear Garden Hill as the site for a huge condominium complex. Later, a large office park was planned by another developer for Brister's Hill, just across Route 2 from the pond's northeastern flank. Either project would have compromised the pond; together, they would have destroyed the integrity of the woods surrounding it, woods that Thoreau treasured and that Concord residents still walk in and enjoy.

A local group, the Thoreau Country Conservation Alliance, began the fight against the Bear Garden Hill condos; Don Henley joined the cause in 1990 and established the Walden Woods Project, contributed and raised millions of dollars, and eventually conserved both sites and many acres more in Concord and nearby Lincoln.

Today, Concord has conserved a surprising amount of undeveloped woodland. Many of the places where Thoreau and Emerson used to roam are safe. A century and a half after his death, Henry David Thoreau is alive and well in Concord.

— — —

Henry lived by the shores of Walden Pond for slightly more than two years. But he walked in the Concord woods almost every day of his adult life. For years and years, he tirelessly, relentlessly trod the pretty, undramatic hills and woods and swamps and fields of Concord. His journal is a record of those and other journeys. In those familiar haunts and vistas, his imagination flourished, along with his powers of perception and understanding, and he discovered new worlds, filled with meaning. Over his relatively short lifetime, he transcribed that information into his journal, all thirty-nine volumes of it. And then he mined those journals for sections of *Walden* and his lectures and essays. Throughout, his writings are packed with the insights that he drew from the Concord groves and hills, a lifetime of walking and observation, day and night.

We descend Bear Garden Hill to the banks of the Sudbury River, where Ginger Lang discovers May apples blooming on the floor of the forest. We all stop and admire the pretty, green, umbrella-like plant and its pure white, downward-facing blossoms. Would Thoreau have seen the ancestors of this flower?

To a large extent, his voluminous journal is the record of his walks around Concord. He walked just about every afternoon, all afternoon, exploring every nook and cranny of the town, its farmlands and wild lands, taking note of the plants and animals he saw there, writing down his own thoughts.

"I think that I cannot preserve my health and spirits, unless I spend four hours a day at least—and it is commonly more than that—sauntering through the woods and over the hills and fields, absolutely free from all worldly engagements," he wrote in the essay "Walking."

In his journal, Thoreau commented on the sluggish, langorous nature of the Sudbury River, calling it "a succession of bays," and adding, "There is just stream enough for a flow of thought; that is all."

However, as we walk alongside it, the river is high and fast, engorged by recent heavy rains. A couple of houses and docks stand on the opposite shore and, downriver, there's a low bridge where the Sudbury Road crosses.

"Thoreau sees people as part of the landscape," Jayne notes, reminding us that the Transcendentalists believed that nature was an extension of the mind, and that Emerson had written, "The water reflects heaven because my mind does."

Transcendentalists were American literary Romantics, a group who gathered around Emerson, the leading public intellectual of his era. Thoreau, born in Concord, became Emerson's friend and chief protégé. In his early career, he imitated Emerson's thought and style—and, according to some, even Emerson's long nose!

But as he grew and matured, Thoreau became his own man. Instead of imitating Emerson or making Transcendentalist points, he came to savor nature more for its own sake, and to record the natural life around Concord more scientifically—though he sometimes fretted that viewing nature scientifically compromised his ability to see its deeper meanings and write poetically about its phenomena.

He became a skilled field biologist, largely self-taught. His family, especially his younger sister, Sophia, helped him and to some degree shared his passion. It was Sophia—intelligent, plain, and deeply devoted to "brother Henry"—who in May of 1853 brought home to her brother the blossom of a wild azalea he had never before seen in Concord. He went off on a long and complicated search for the shrub, eventually found it, and recorded the incident and the plant triumphantly in his journal.

His later journal writings suggest that he was attempting to research and construct a master-calendar of all the natural phenomena in Concord. He died before the project could be completed, and some scholars speculate that as he became more meticulously scientific in his later years, the magic went out of his writing and his observations. Current research disputes that contention, and holds that Thoreau never lost his sense of wonder or his ability to convey it through his writing. Jayne agrees:

"He spends the 1850s doing his chronology [of natural phenomena]," she tells us. "The more he knows, the more miraculous it all is."

Our little group skirts the bottom of Fair Haven Hill. We can't go to the top of it for whatever view the current forest may allow because it is privately owned, the site of some exclusive houses: no trespassing here. We move along the river's edge and climb to Grape Cliffs, a sunny outcropping of rocks with a nice view of the river and the opposite hills. It was one of Henry's favorite places, and we plop ourselves down on the rocks to eat our sandwiches. It was just about this time of year—late May—when he wrote, sitting in this same spot:

"The world can never be more beautiful than now, for, combined with the tender fresh green, you have this remarkable clearness of the air. I doubt if the landscape will be any greener. . . . Those great fields of green affect me as did those early green blades by the Corner Spring, —like a fire flaming up from the earth."

The view from these cliffs is pleasant, not dramatic. They are about fifty to sixty feet high, a series of rounded rock ledges above the Sudbury River. Fair Haven Bay, where the river broadens off to the south, is a gleaming expanse of water almost as large as Walden Pond.

Even though Thoreau would have seen grander landscapes in the mountains of the north, he loved this one. It inspired some of his best journal entries. Jayne reads one of them, perhaps chosen to remind us that the forested landscape we see today was, in Thoreau's time, largely deforested—cutover meadows with a few woodlots.

"This afternoon, being on Fair Haven Hill, I heard the sound of a saw, and soon after from the Cliff saw two men sawing down a noble pine beneath, about forty rods off. I resolved to watch it till it fell, the last of a dozen or more which were left when the forest was cut and for fifteen years have waved in solitary majesty over the sprout-land. I saw them like beavers or insects gnawing at the trunk of this noble tree, the diminutive manikins with their cross-cut saw which could scarcely span it. It towered up a hundred feet as I afterward found by measurement, one of the tallest probably in the township and straight as an arrow, but slanting a little toward the hillside, its top seen against the frozen river and the hills of Conantum. I watch closely to see when it begins to move.

"Now the sawers stop, and with an ax open it a little on the side toward which it leans, that it may break the faster. And now their saw goes again. Now surely it is going; it is inclined one-quarter of the quadrant, and, breathless, I expect its crashing fall. But no, I was mistaken; it has not moved an inch; it stands at the same angle as at first. It is fifteen minutes yet to its fall. Still its branches wave in the wind, as if it were destined to stand for a century, and the wind soughs through its needles as of yore; it is still a forest tree, the most majestic tree that waves over Musketaquid. The silvery sheen of the sunlight is reflected from its needles; it still affords an inaccessible crotch for the squirrel's nest; not a lichen has forsaken its mast-like stem, its raking mast,—the hill is the hulk.

"Now, now's the moment! The manikins at its base are fleeing from their crime. They have dropped the guilty saw and axe. How slowly and majestically it starts! as if it were only swayed by a summer breeze, and would return without a sigh to its location in the air. And now it fans the hillside with its fall, and it lies down to its bed in the valley, from which it is never to rise, as softly as a feather, folding its green mantle about it like a warrior, as if, tired of standing, it embraced the earth with silent joy, returning its elements to the dust again.

"But hark! there you only saw, but did not hear. There now comes up a deafening crash to these rocks, advertising you that even trees do not die without a groan. It rushes to embrace the earth and mingle its elements with the dust. And now all is still, once more and forever, both to eye and ear. . . .

"A plant which it has taken two centuries to perfect, rising by slow stages into the heavens, has this afternoon ceased to exist. . . . Why does not the village bell sound a knell? I hear no knell tolled. I see no procession of mourners in the streets, or the woodland aisles. The squirrel has leaped to another tree; the hawk has circled further off, and has now settled upon a new eyrie, but the woodman is preparing [to] lay his axe at the root of that also."

I can imagine Thoreau, sitting not far from where we are sitting, watching, fuming in anger at the cutting of the great pine, stalking back to town and angrily scribbling those passionate, beautiful words in his journal. We look across the rain-swollen river to "the hills of Conantum," now completely forested with second- or maybe third-growth trees. There are no hundred-foot pines there now. A few houses peek out from within the new green foliage.

The name Conantum, Jayne tells us, was one of Henry's personal jokes. Scholars for years puzzled over the term: was Conantum an old Colonial site? A Native American village? or what? Then someone found that the land Henry was referring to throughout his journals as "Conantum" belonged to a farmer named Ebeneezer Conant. End of mystery.

Today, Conantum is not a farm but a residential neighborhood. It still bears the name given by Thoreau as an in-joke. When it was subdivided in the 1950s the development caused something of a stir in conservative Yankee Concord because the houses were being put up by college liberals from the Boston area. And the houses were prefabricated structures thought not to be up to the architectural standards of elite Concord.

"Today, that's some of the best real estate in Concord," one of our party notes.

As we sit on the rocks, picnicking in a row, a chunky middle-aged man in red shorts comes jogging by on the trail. He begins bowing repeatedly toward the river—touching his toes, stretching, or something. After a few repetitions, he jogs off through the forest.

"What was that?" one of the women asks with an arched eyebrow. "Showing off?"

"I guess we were supposed to be impressed," another says. "Oh, what an awesome display of masculine vigor!"

Everyone laughs, and we gather up our lunch odds and ends, slip on our packs, and continue along the trail. A great crested flycatcher is shrieking in the woods across Fair Haven Bay. Ginger stops to point out rue-anemone, a small, delicate spring wildflower, blooming right beside the trail.

We walk on—to the Andromeda Ponds, past swampy Well Meadow, through green and grassy Pleasant Meadow, alongside Heywood

Brook—all places known intimately by Thoreau, savored in his walks, mentioned in his journals. Jayne helps us deepen our appreciation for them by reading passages from the journals as we proceed. The Andromeda Ponds seem a dank, shady, slightly spooky place to me and, though he liked them, Thoreau could apparently feel the same way, commenting in one December passage, "what a horrible shaggy forest the Andromeda Ponds were yesterday." But he often savored the darker moods of nature, and the plant andromeda (bog rosemary), for which these little boggy ponds were named, was one of his favorites. At his funeral, Louisa May Alcott placed a wreath of andromeda among the wildflowers on his casket.

— — —

Almost all of these places that Thoreau loved are identifiable today. Many of them have been conserved and can be visited—if you know the paths. In some places—Pleasant Meadow, for example—the land is in private hands, but enlightened owners have kept the property as it was 150 years ago.

We wind our way back toward Walden Pond. After clambering across the railroad tracks once more, we come to Heywood's Meadow—an attractive wild bog—where we stop for a rest. It is late afternoon. We sit above the bog on sun-warmed pine needles, and Jayne reads us an 1850 journal passage in which Thoreau describes a disturbance in this bog and discovers that a snapping turtle is devouring a still-living horned pout. "I had no idea that there was so much going on in Heywood's meadow," Henry wrote.

There's still quite a bit going on there today. We rest on the pine-studded bank above the marshy water and watch a flock of tree swallows work the bug-filled air. On the far side, beyond the thin line of open water, there's a flowering rhodora—a wild azalea with light pink-purple blossoms on its bare branches. Thoreau wrote about this plant often and clearly liked it. It was about this time of year in 1854 that he noted,

"The splendid rhodora now sets the swamps on fire with its masses of rich color. . . . I see the light purple of the rhodora enlivening the edges of the swamps—another color the sun wears."

Heywood's Meadow is a rough, pretty place; as we rest and soak up the late-afternoon sun, I quietly marvel that its wild beauty is still here and undisturbed for us to enjoy, 150 years after Thoreau did the same thing. We are within twenty miles of Boston, within two miles of downtown Concord, and within a couple hundred yards of the railroad tracks and the sprawling 21st-century network of highways and phone lines—the ganglia and nervous tissue of our driven society. Yet here we sit, not saying much, savoring the perceptions and thoughts—the mind, really—of Concord's resident oddball genius as we watch the swallows soar and dive above the sedges. How lovely. How unusual.

This is at least a part of what Thoreau had in mind when he declared, "In Wildness is the preservation of the world." He loved wilderness—a different animal—and went long distances to find it, into northern Maine and up the flanks of Katahdin, for example. But he discovered the everyday wildness of Nature, Mother Earth, the Tao—whatever we may choose to call it—at Walden Pond and in the quiet meadows and bogs and woodlots of the Concord countryside. He plumbed the depths of the universe in his extended back yard, and never tired of what he found there.

And that, of course, is one of the hallmarks of genius.

—— —— ——

The next day, Sunday, I go to visit Flint's Pond. Thoreau wrote an outraged diatribe in Walden against "the unclean and stupid farmer" who owned this pond, and legend has it that outburst was written because Henry had been denied permission to build a hut there (this was prior to his Walden Pond sojourn). Whatever his reason, his anger at the owner of Flint's Pond is real. He describes the owner, punning, as "some skin-flint," who loved money better than anything and regarded even the wild ducks that swam on the pond as trespassers, whose fingers had grown into horny talons from the habit of grasping:

"I go not there to see him nor to hear of him . . . who never loved it [the pond]; who never protected it, who never spoke a good word for it, nor thanked God that he had made it . . . who thought only of its money value; whose presence perchance cursed all the shore; who exhausted all the land around it, and would fain have exhausted the waters within it; who regretted only that it was not English hay or cranberry meadow . . . and would have drained and sold it for the mud at its bottom."

In short, Henry let Farmer Flint have a taste of his pique. He nonetheless wrote affectionately of Flint's Pond as "our greatest lake or inland sea," and noted that he often walked there through the woods surrounding it for recreation. A trail links Walden Pond with Flint's Pond, and there are walking trails beside the pond and through the nearby woods today. It is now known as Sandy Pond (a name change that would have pleased Thoreau, obviously). It is a public water supply for the town of Lincoln: no boating or swimming allowed. But there is a nice swath of conserved woods along the pond's western shore. The public trails, though minimally marked, are easy to find.

I spend a pleasant couple of hours, binoculars in hand, birding in the spring woods, the sunlit pond glimmering through the trees. In a small field by the lake, tree swallows dive and soar, then perch in the top of a lone pine tree. There's a yellow warbler, a song sparrow, and a catbird, all quite busy in in the viny tangles next to the pond. There's also plenty of poison ivy, so I make my way back into the woods.

An oriole is calling from a tall oak tree, but I can't get him to come out. However, a scarlet tanager in the forest canopy does respond, and I get a good look at the bright red little bird with natty black wings as he hops about in the treetops, singing his hoarse, loud song. Henry liked the tanager's brightness. He noted that it reversed the color scheme of the red-winged blackbird, and declared that it "most takes the eye of any bird. It flies through the green foliage as if it would ignite the leaves."

He made this journal entry on May 21, 1853, exactly—to the day—153 years before my visit to these woods.

I've noticed that the trails in Concord and Lincoln are minimally marked and not promoted to the public at all. They are obviously intended to be used and enjoyed primarily by local people—not the hoi polloi from Boston, or Vermont. No matter. In my two hours in these woods I meet a grand total of one other person—a woman runner, who smiles and says nothing as she passes.

It's lovely in the woods—the fresh green of the new leaves, the sunlight filtering through, making patterns on the forest floor, gleaming off the pond, the birds vigorously singing away with all the abandon of spring. The forest feels filled to its topmost branches with life, with wildness.

I leave reluctantly. There's one or two more stops I want to make before I leave Concord and head home. Driving back into town from Flint's Pond, I pass through acres of undeveloped swampy forest, filled with birds and mosquitos. How nice. Henry might even drop out of character and be pleased.

The Concord Museum is open, even though it's Sunday. Sabbath observance is in decline. That would please him also.

Inside, there's a Thoreau room, with a nice bust, and quotations from Walden and the journals. The actual desk and bedstead from Henry's little cabin—the only house he ever owned—are on display. They are about as plain and simple as pieces of furniture can be, and do not conjure up Thoreau for me at all.

But here, in a glass case, is Henry's flute—a handsome varnished wooden flute engraved with Henry's name and that of his father, John. I can imagine him in his skiff, out on Walden Pond, serenading the schools of perch gathered around him, the flute's mellow voice echoing across the moonlit pond.

And here, donated by his ever-patient, ever-caring sister, Sophia, is "the last pen brother Henry wrote with." It was Sophia who believed in Henry all his life, Sophia who nurtured him and read to him during his final illness, Sophia who (with Ellery Channing) helped organize and gather his articles and lectures, and helped usher *The Maine Woods* and *Cape Cod* to publication after her beloved brother's death. It was Sophia, also, who helped keep Henry's memory alive until the recognition he deserved finally caught up with him.

And today it is Sophia who lies buried beside "brother Henry," in the family plot in Sleepy Hollow Cemetery.

— — —

Thoreau was buried on Author's Ridge in Sleepy Hollow in the spring of 1862, after he died of the family ailment, tuberculosis. It is a beautiful place, full of birds and flowers, one of the first land-scaped park-cemeteries in America. Author's Ridge is toward the back, the rim of an irregular half-bowl that encompasses much of the cemetery. Thoreau is buried with the rest of his family on one edge of the curving ridge, across the path from the grave of his friend Nathaniel Hawthorne.

A large stone in the center of the Thoreau family plot is inscribed with the names and dates of each family member and smaller stones mark each individual grave. Henry and Sophia lie next to one another, an arrangement doubtless requested by Sophia, the loyal younger sister who adored her older brother. The graves command a pleasing view of the landscaped stones and the shrubs and flowers spread out below Author's Ridge. If Henry could see the plantings, he could probably supply the Latin names of most of them.

A few steps along the ridge lie the stones of the Alcotts, and farther along is the large, rough-hewn boulder marking Emerson's grave, with headstones of the other Emerson family members surrounding it. Just down the hill in the natural bowl sheltered by Author's Ridge is the grave of Edward Hoar, Thoreau's friend who financed his trip to the White Mountains and accompanied him on his longest canoe trip through the wilds of northern Maine.

Here lie the last mortal remains of the New England literary renaissance; the immortal portions are enshrined in libraries and college English departments across the country. Visitors climb the ridge and move quietly among the sun-dappled grave markers. The birds singing in the trees are louder than their hushed voices. Pebbles and a few pennies have been left on the authors' graves in tribute, and some people have left notes for their favorite authors. "Louisa May Alcott!" one young fan has written. "I love all of your books. I listen to the *Little Women* tapes before I go to bed. You are a great writer!" It is signed simply: "Emma."

There are no notes on Henry's modest grave today. But there are several pebbles and, instead of pennies, an oak leaf, a few pinecones, a struggling geranium with a single red blossom. He was not a particularly humble man, but he hated ostentation. And so it is appropriate that his stone is one of the smallest in the cemetery.

Gradually the village murmur subsided, and we seemed to be embarked on the placid current of our dreams, floating from past to future as silently as one awakes to fresh morning or evening thoughts. We glided noiselessly down the stream, occasionally driving a pickerel from the covert of the pads, or a bream from her nest, and the smaller bittern now and then sailed away on sluggish wings from some recess in the shore, or the larger lifted itself out of the long grass at our approach, and carried its precious legs away to deposit them in a place of safety.

—A Week on the Concord and Merrimack Rivers

3

A Day on the Concord & Merrimack Rivers

enry David Thoreau grew up beside the Concord River. From his earliest days, he fished it, swam in it, rowed on it, and collected plants along its banks.

In 1839, when he was twenty-two, he and his older brother John took an ambitious two-week trip on the Concord and Merrimack rivers, northward into the wild White Mountains of New Hampshire. They rowed down the Concord River to its junction with the Merrimack. There they turned north and rowed upstream as far as they could go, which turned out to be a point above the Amoskeag Falls, near Concord, New Hampshire. From there, they hiked into the mountains, to the headwaters of the Merrimack's main tributary, the Pemigewasset River. Next, they climbed "Agiocochook"—Mount Washington, the highest peak in New England. And then they hiked back to their boat and rode the winds homeward, using their sail—which, like the boat, they had made themselves.

At the time, the adventure was little more than a late-summer outing for two lads testing their young manhood. However, for Henry, it later became much more than that.

The Concord was and is a placid, sluggish river. Today, only the fourteen or so miles from the point near Concord village where the Assabet and Sudbury rivers join, northeast to Lowell, where it merges with the Merrimack, is called the Concord River. Historically, the long arm that curves southward through Sudbury toward Framingham and is now called the Sudbury River was part of the Concord. That is why Henry was correct when he described the river as being fifty miles in length.

The Merrimack—the much larger main stem of the watershed—is a big, powerful river, one of the great rivers of New England. It is 110 miles long and drains some five thousand square miles of central and southern New Hampshire and northeastern Massachusetts. It begins in Franklin, New Hampshire, as a fast-flowing mountain stream, but by the time it pours its waters into the Atlantic Ocean near Plum Island and Newburyport, it is a grand tidal estuary, in places more than a half-mile across.

The Concord is one of its smaller tributaries, but has a rich history. Its Native American name, "Musketaquid," or "grass-ground river," refers to the broad meadows that once lined its banks and drew both Native American and European settlers there.

"It will be Grass-ground River as long as grass grows and water runs here," Thoreau wrote. "It will be Concord River only while men lead peaceable lives on its banks."

That comment is from the opening paragraphs of *A Week on the Concord and Merrimack Rivers*, the book he wrote chronicling his 1839 river excursion—and a great deal more—in 1845, more than six years after the actual trip and three years after John's tragic death.

Neither the Concord nor the Merrimack was a wild river in Thoreau's day, nor are they in ours. Though Thoreau followed the Romantic literary conventions of his day and described the landscape in predominately pastoral terms, he was too good a writer (and too honest a man) to gloss over the fact that even as he and John rowed through it, the Merrimack Valley was developing into a major industrial complex, one of America's early manufacturing centers.

"See how this river was devoted from the first to the service of manufactures," he wrote. "Instead of the scream of a fish-hawk scaring the fishes, is heard the whistle of the steam-engine, arousing a country to its progress."

In 1839, Lowell, Massachusetts, where the two rivers joined, was a burgeoning factory town, spinning cloth of cotton and wool. The entire Merrimack Valley was a vital artery in the nascent industrialization of New England. Mills and factories were being built as far upstream as the little village of Manchester, New Hampshire, where the Amoskeag Falls had been harnessed to provide yet more water power. Bricks made from the clayey soils of the upper Merrimack Valley were shipped downstream on sailing canal boats, along with lumber, iron ore, and other necessaries of the dawning industrial age.

Even as the Thoreau brothers rowed and towed their hand-built dory upstream, the pastoral landscape that they camped in was being transformed. The success of their trip, in fact, depended upon some of the river's industrial infrastructure. Canals at Billerica, Lowell, Hooksett, and elsewhere made their journey upriver possible—or, at the very least, much, much easier. Just above the falls at Billerica, on the second day of their trip, they left the Concord River and entered a system of canals that they followed for six miles.

"As we did not care to loiter in this part of our voyage, while one ran along the tow-path [beside the canal] drawing the boat by a cord, the other kept it off the shore with a pole," Henry wrote. "We accomplished the whole distance in little more than an hour." They eventually were locked down into the Merrimack above Lowell, and then made use of the Merrimack River's canals several times, as their journey progressed onward.

They also met canal boats, and even got a tow-ride upstream with one of them for a distance. But Henry observed that by 1845, the day of canals and boats on the river was passing. "Since our voyage the railroad on the bank has been extended, and there is now but little boating on the Merrimack." He added that the locks and canals themselves were wearing out because there was no longer enough floating traffic to sustain their use.

Thus, Thoreau was witnessing—and participating in—the transition from one technological era to another, even as the pace of New England's industrialization continued and quickened.

Out early in search of decent coffee—a finicky addiction that Henry Thoreau would have scorned—I drive into the first quick-stop I can find on the non-historic outskirts of historic Concord. As I fumble with the multiple coffee urns, a lanky blond guy in his forties approaches me. "Out for a big day on the river?" he asks.

"Hope so," I respond.

He must have noticed the canoe on top of my car. It would have been hard to miss. It's at least thirty years old, more than sixteen feet long, and mud-brown in color; its fiberglass is honorably battle-scarred with dings and scratches from various rocks and river obstacles, and patched in several places. It's a big canoe on a little car: bow and stern extend beyond the front and rear bumpers of my small station wagon.

The blond guy fishes the river a lot, wants to make sure I stop at Old North Bridge, the famous Concord battle site where colonials won their first Revolutionary War victory. "It's worth seeing," he says.

Apparently the river is still important to the people who live beside it.

Coffee and sandwiches for lunch secured, I head back to the motel and roust Ethan, my son and voluntary bearer, out of bed. Like his mother, he's a night person and normally sleeps late. He doesn't complain much. We grab a bite at the free motel breakfast (a term of art if ever there was one) and head for our date on the river.

At the landing below the Lowell Street Bridge, it takes the two of us—father and son—to get the old canoe's seventy-five pounds off the car. My back will no longer manage it alone, so I'm thankful for Ethan's company. Plus, he's fun to be with. One of the great benefits of parenthood is doing things with your adult children.

We arrive at the Lowell Street Bridge and lug the old brown canoe down to the river's edge. It's a Mad River Malecite, one of the first carefully designed downriver boats when I bought it years ago. I have paddled many a mile in the old scow and I love it—but not without reservation. It's both graceful and stable in the water but, because it's fiberglass, it's heavy out of water. Its original wood gunwales are long gone, replaced by shapely ash gunwales that I installed after the first set more or less gave up the ghost. It's what I get for taking a downriver boat into whitewater. Nevertheless, we've been down a lot of rivers together. Time for one more trip.

More people pull into the parking lot below the bridge and drop off boats, mostly bright-colored plastic kayaks. Soon there are ten of us: eight kayaks and the two-man brown Malecite.

We are booked into a daylong paddle sponsored by the Merrimack River Watershed Council, a conservation group dedicated to restoring the ecological health of the entire sprawling multi-river system of which the Merrimack is the main stem. Paddling tours like this are an important part of what they do. Our leader, Julie Smith, says the trips are educational— and a subtle way of building a constituency for the Merrimack and its tributaries. "We want to show people that the river's there, it's free, it's multi-use," she says. Julie, tall and athletic, takes her responsibilities as a trip leader seriously. She briefs us carefully on the trip and the Watershed Council, checks to make sure that everyone has a life jacket, and hauls her own kayak out of her van. It's a much-scarred purple "Pyranha"—a tiny whitewater kayak that looks about as long as Julie is tall. It's obvious that our leader has spent time on rivers a lot wilder than the Concord.

It's also becoming obvious that Ethan and I are the shabby country cousins on this trip. The kayaks (with the exception of Julie's) are all pretty new and spiffy looking. Some are long, dagger-like sea kayaks. Others are short and beamy. But they all glow brilliantly as they bob like brightly colored corks—green, yellow, red, orange, blue—in the smooth dark-olive water. Likewise, the gear that goes with them—paddles, lifejackets, and so forth—is all very shiny, colorful, and *au courant* as well. The old beat-up Malecite looks like a relic beside them. It is obvious that paddling technology has advanced radically in the last few years. Fortunately, no one scorns us two Vermonters because of our down-rent appearance.

Kayaks are almost as numerous on the Concord as the bicycles that fill the town's shady, winding back roads. Throughout the day, I count maybe two or three other canoes on the river. There are easily twenty-five or thirty kayaks out, including the eight in our group.

And they are much more nimble on the water than the Mighty Malecite. Ethan and I track downriver very well, but our turns are usually long, graceful arcs, and we need to allow for some drift in navigating each bend in the river. The zippy little kayaks can turn on a dime.

Paddling along downriver, I find myself in close quarters with several kayaks, and come close to a mid-river collision with one—a long red job with a black rudder up-tilted on its pointed red stern. "Oops—reckless driver!" teases its pilot, a pleasant middle-aged blond woman. "That reminds me," she adds. "Did you see that documentary last weekend on public television—on the *Stockholm* and the *Andrea Doria*?"

We had. The collision at sea of the two ocean liners was one of the historic events of my youth. We laugh, and paddle onward.

There's more room now; the river is getting wider. At Lowell Street Bridge it was maybe fifty yards across. But it widens gradually as we go downstream, and is broad, dark, and smooth by the time we approach Great Meadows National Wildlife Refuge. There are big, reedy embayments off to each side and rows of oaks and maples—good-sized trees—overhang the smoothly flowing water.

Here and there painted turtles, in graduated sizes, sun themselves on snags or rocks. A great blue heron rises off the reeds and flies away, looking vaguely prehistoric. Other birds flitter through the trees but, because of the full summer foliage, I can't identify them. Ethan, in the front of the canoe, turns around and grins happily back at me: "Do we have to go back to civilization?"

I know how he feels. Freedom. It is the cry of Thoreau at Walden, of Huckleberry Finn on the Mississippi, of Jim Hawkins on Treasure Island, of Edward Abbey on the Rio Grande—of every escapee from the troubled life of cities and everyday responsibility. Rivers cast a spell.

We enter Great Meadows National Wildlife Refuge. I have been anticipating the sight of the broad open meadows that gave the river its Native American name. Thoreau describes the river and surrounding open lands in *A Week:*

"For the most part, it creeps through broad meadows, adorned with scattered oaks, where the cranberry is found in abundance, covering the ground like a moss-bed . . . while at a greater distance the meadow is skirted with maples, alders, and other fluviatile trees overrun with the grape-vine. . . . Still farther from the stream, on the edge of the firm land, are seen the gray and white dwellings of the inhabitants."

The "row of sunken willows" that Thoreau described still borders the riverbank in many places, but all his longer views are now masked by trees. Very little grass grows beside the "Grass-ground River" these days. Hay is no longer cut there.

A series of dams, built during the 19th century and into the 20th, have repeatedly raised the river's water level, turning the broad meadows into a forested wetland. The process was already underway in Thoreau's time. He writes in *A Week* that the once-open fields are being flooded by a dam at Billerica, ten miles downstream, and that the factories and canals at Lowell have put an end to the historic migration of the shad up the Concord. Even though he writes in the elevated, literary style of the day, using "thee" and "thy" diction that he would later abandon for plainer, more direct language, his sympathies are clearly with the fish whose natural spawning cycle has been broken by the dams.

"Poor shad!" declares Thoreau. "Where is thy redress?" He advises the fish to "keep a stiff fin then, and stem all the tides thou mayst meet." He also hints at a little 19th-century ecotage: "I for one am with thee, and who knows what may avail a crow-bar against that Billerica dam?"

We paddle on through the refuge. It's still a pretty river with lots of wildlife, even though its broader views and the historic meadows are gone. The blue-flowering pickerel weed and buttonbush that Thoreau describes are still blossoming, but I look in vain for the bright scarlet flash of cardinal flowers, which he said were blooming profusely about this time of year.

We stop for lunch at Carlisle Bridge and—oh horrors!—the Mighty Malecite is shipping water. In addition to being old and unfashionable, it's leaky! My extra shirt and bird book are floating quietly in the canoe's bilge. Fortunately, one of the women paddlers reaches into her spiffy plastic kayak and draws forth—a spiffy plastic water pump! It quickly dumps overboard the two or three gallons of water we have taken on.

We settle down at the boat launch beside the bridge and eat sandwiches from the quick-stop and cherries, shipped from Washington State. As we chat among ourselves, a little German shepherd puppy from a docked motorboat frisks around, winning lots of attention from our group. Across the river, the foundation of the historic bridge that spanned this river in the 1840s is still visible.

On down the river our little flotilla goes. The Concord is much broader now, a long, winding lake, and we periodically encounter motorboats, usually trolling fishing lines. And then, incongruously, one fast-moving boat appears, towing a water-skier. Our paddlecraft bob in the wake after each boat passes.

We pass under bridges large and small as we paddle along. Some are historic. Most are quiet, shady passages that make the slow current barely visible, and which we glide silently through. But near the end of the day, we approach the Route 3 bridge, a major thoroughfare, and it is something else, a big span, high above the river, decorated on each side with non-functional, aluminum spandrel arches. As we pass silently under it, the bridge literally howls from the constant stream of traffic it carries across the river.

Not long afterwards, we reach North Billerica, where we paddle to the river's edge, drag our boats up a steep bank, hoist them over a waist-high steel fence and lift them onto the cars we dropped off there several hours earlier.

It's been a long day and Ethan and I are sunburned and more than a little tired. We seek out Italian food, stuff ourselves with pasta, tomato sauce, and beer, and sleep soundly in our motel campsite.

—— —— ——

One of the reasons Thoreau went to Walden Pond was to write about the Concord and Merrimack rivers. It had been six years since the trip, and three years since John Thoreau had died tragically of tetanus (lockjaw). He had nicked a finger while shaving and, though he had bandaged the wound, he promptly contracted the disease and died, painfully, in Henry's arms.

John was Henry's closest friend, and his sudden death left his younger brother so completely devastated that Henry developed a sympathetic case of lockjaw that lasted a week and deeply frightened his family. Depression—from John's death and probably also from several failed enterprises of his own—began to haunt him. And so when Emerson offered him the use of his land on the north shore of Walden Pond, Henry decided to build a cabin there. Part of his purpose was to memorialize John by writing up an account of their trip together to the headwaters of the Merrimack River.

He was working on early drafts of *Walden* at the same time. But unlike *Walden*, *A Week on the Concord and Merrimack Rivers* was not successful, either commercially or artistically.

The book was carrying some heavy baggage from the beginning. In addition to being a memorial to John, it was Henry's first book-length project, his "learner" book. As Thoreau revised it, it grew from a fairly compact account of the camping trip into a sprawling, four-hundred-page compendium of his thoughts, opinions, and reading on everything from the laws of morality to the fishes that inhabit the Concord River. Like *Walden*, much of the book was mined from Thoreau's voluminous journals. Unlike *Walden*, Thoreau seems hardly to have edited *A Week* at all. Readings from and references to local history, Greek mythology, Chaucer's poetry, the writings of Homer, Shakespeare, and a great deal more are inserted into his account, as he and John row up and down the two rivers. Apparently eager to display his Harvard education (and perhaps smarting because of his early failures as a schoolmaster and a journalist) he tosses in disquisitions on ancient civilizations from around the globe and a variety of historic personages literally from A to Z—King Arthur to Zoroaster.

There's more digression in *A Week* than actual narrative about the trip—much more. The result is an awkward, overstuffed book that lurches from place to place and subject to subject in a cumbersome and disconcerting way.

"We occasionally rested in the shade of a maple or a willow, and drew forth a melon for our refreshment, while we contemplated at our leisure the lapse of the river and of human life," begins a typical digression. "And as that current, with its floating twigs and leaves, so did all things pass in review before us. . . ."

You never know just where Thoreau will head off to after an introduction like that. In this case (in the chapter "Monday") it's a long discussion on the need for reform in human affairs. Not specifically, but generally, vaguely.

Thoreau declares that "the restless class of reformers" is to be avoided, then offers suggestions on the wisdom of patience ("All good abides with him who waiteth wisely. . . ."), on the superficiality of politics, on the tediousness of the law, on the pitfalls of over-writing ("The language of excitement is at best picturesque. . . ."), on the need for humility, and the suspect nature of conscience. He proceeds with a critique of Sophocles' *Antigone*, with praise for the "conservatism" of Indian mystics, with a tip of the hat to Christianity, and concludes with the suggestion that it would be "worthy of the age" to print a collection of spiritual writings from "the several nations, the Chinese, the Hindoos, the Persians, the Hebrews, and others, as the Scripture of mankind. . . . This is a work which Time will surely edit, reserved to crown the labors of the printing press," he declares.

After a brief return to the river, in which he and John hitch a short ride upriver on a canal boat, Henry plunges into an extended essay on the *Bhagavad-Gita* and Indian literature. And more digressions follow.

The longest of these, a twenty-page set piece on friendship, is probably both Thoreau's climactic memorial to his brother, and an exploration of his complex relationship with Emerson. It is very heavy going, abstract and at times intellectually tortured.

Overall, *A Week* is a tendentious, episodic, fragmented book. Which is too bad, because there is a shorter, better book hidden within it: the story of the river camping trip and hike, sweet and simple. Despite the book's flawed, wandering structure, it contains many beautifully effective passages—almost always when Thoreau writes about the river, the surrounding countryside, or the events of the journey itself.

His descriptions of the landscape through which he and John pass are often luminous and compelling, Transcendentalist writing at its best. He can also coin amusing and effective figures of speech, such as when he and John bedded down and slept amidst the singing of crickets: "A thousand little artisans beat on their anvils all night long."

He seems to have a special sensitivity and affection for the subtle pleasures of camping out—perhaps because he was living close to nature at Walden Pond when he wrote much of the book. Here is his description of a night camping by the Merrimack on the return trip. He wakes in the night when the wind fitfully blows the flaps of his tent:

"With our heads so low in the grass, we heard the river whirling and sucking, and lapsing downward, kissing the shore as it went, sometimes rippling louder than usual, and again its mighty current making only a slight limpid trickling sound, as if our water-pail had sprung a leak, and the water were flowing into the grass by our side. The wind, rustling the oaks and hazels, impressed us like a wakeful and inconsiderate person up at midnight, moving about, and putting things to rights, occasionally stirring up whole drawers full of leaves at a puff. There seemed to be a great haste and preparation throughout Nature, as for a distinguished visitor; all her aisles had to be swept in the night, by a thousand hand-maidens, and a thousand pots to be boiled for the next day's feasting;—such a whispering bustle, as if ten thousand fairies made their fingers fly, silently sewing at the new carpet with which the earth was to be clothed, and the new drapery which was to adorn the trees. And then the wind would lull and die away, and we like it fell asleep again."

Unfortunately, such passages are relatively rare. The tone of most of *A Week* is didactic, preachy. In *Walden*, Thoreau eventually learns to listen to his world—the natural world—and relates to us what he has learned by that listening; in *A Week*, he seems more intent on showing us how much he knows.

Thoreau had predictable trouble in finding a publisher for the heavily freighted book, and eventually had to guarantee the cost of the printing himself. Once published, in 1849, reviews were decidedly mixed. Several reviewers liked portions of *A Week*, but were scandalized by the author's flagrant Transcendentalism and lack of respect for traditional churchly Christianity. Even though Emerson did much to promote this first book by his young friend, he noted that its narrative formed "a very slender thread for such big beads and ingots as are strung on it." And poet and editor James Russell Lowell, who also was at least partly kind, commented in his review of the book that readers were "bid to a river party, not to be preached at."

When *A Week* did not sell, Thoreau was obliged to purchase the hundreds of remaindered copies and have them carted to Concord. By then, Henry was living at home with his parents again. He carried them in armloads upstairs to his third-floor bedroom. The book's failure was a crushing blow to Thoreau, but he was able to comment wryly on the situation:

"I have now a library of nearly nine hundred volumes, over seven hundred of which I wrote myself."

He gave away individual copies to his friends and visitors for the rest of his life.

T he morning after our Concord excursion was a Sunday. Ethan and I packed up and went off to explore the Merrimack River. We spent the day ferreting out places mentioned by Thoreau and historic sites, both official and unofficial. What we found was a river being translated from industry to recreation—from a combination superhighway and sewer into a paddlers' retreat.

Plenty of evidence of the Merrimack's industrial past still exists—in the Lowell National Historical Park and other parks that consciously preserve that past, and in isolated shreds and remnants of 19th-century industrial infrastructure along the river itself. Even our casual survey spotted collapsing piles of stone that once were canal locks, iron bolts and D-rings still anchored in rock, and sections of stone riprap a century old on the river banks.

The water in the river is cleaner today than it has been for more than a century. Though the Thoreaus drank directly from the Merrimack in 1839, I had no desire to follow suit in 2006, since the river now carries the treated sewage effluent of several hundred thousand people. Among other things.

Still, there's a big difference between treated sewage effluent, which is clear and dissipates quickly in the flowing stream, and raw sewage— which is what the river used to carry, along with millions of gallons of untreated industrial waste.

"There was a time you didn't even want to drive across the river, it smelled so bad," said Gwen Whitbeck, who organizes river trips for the Merrimack River Watershed Council. Referring to a major tributary, she added, "The color of the Nashua River would change from day to day, depending on what they were making."

A river that changes color is memorable. Several people mentioned the phenomenon to me, and the Nashua River Watershed Association website also documents that sad fact.

The river valley's amalgam of 19th-century industry, which Thoreau saw the beginnings of, was all but defunct by the latter half of the 20th century. For years, the textile mills stood like empty ghosts of an earlier New England alongside river banks, scattered throughout the entire Merrimack watershed. Now they are being restored and reused as historical parks, shops, restaurants. The federal Clean Water Act and the work of local environmental organizations like the Merrimack River Watershed Council have removed the sewage and most of the waste from the river and, amazingly enough, the rivers are recovering. One of the great environmental success stories of the past half-century has been the cleaning up of New England's rivers. Henry himself would be pleased. It is something to feel good about.

The river today is recognizable as the river that he described in the

1840s. No longer stained with dye or clouded with sewage, it is once again, "not a dead but a living stream. . . . It has a swift current, and, in this part of its course, a clayey bottom, almost no weeds, and comparatively few fishes. We looked down into its yellow water with the more curiosity, who were accustomed to the Nile-like blackness of the [Concord] river."

At Tyngsborough, Merrimack, Reeds Ferry, and Manchester, Ethan and I looked down into the flowing water and found it once again clear and yellowish. At Merrimack, where a small brook flows into the river through a concrete underpass, we could see the remnant tatters left in tree branches above us by the spring floods, when the river was not clear or yellowish, but roiled and opaque brown. They were a good three feet above our heads.

Despite the bankside tangles of scrub brush and poison ivy, at more than one place we spotted distant kayaks, slipping through the water like bright-colored alligators. Searching for the river in the neighborhoods of south Manchester, we were hailed by a friendly man in a fatigue jacket who saw the canoe on our car and guessed that we wanted to paddle that section of river. He directed us to his right-of-way, and we followed it down to a sandy bank and the broad river. Just downriver were the crumbling stone remains of a set of locks that would have helped Thoreau surmount the Amoskeag Falls. Across the river, through a scrim of trees, we could hear the interstate, roaring.

Actually, for most of its length between Lowell and Manchester, the Merrimack seems secluded and quiet—a watery corridor paradoxically now apart from the bustle of contemporary New Hampshire. "The banks are generally steep and high, with a narrow interval reaching back to the hills," Thoreau wrote. Today's roads and developments are mostly situated on that intervale or those hills, and so the steep banks now block out most of the 21st century.

The water in the river gets cleaner every year, according to Gwen Whitbeck. Because of that improvement and the secluded nature of the river channel, paddlers and picknickers seek it out.

"It's so different now," Gwen said. "People actually use the river. And the towns along the watershed—Lowell, Lawrence, Nashua—really promote it. An awful lot of work has gone into it—greenways and river walks."

Whitbeck has noticed people upstream sitting in beach chairs on hot days, right in the Merrimack and the Pemigewasset. The river that once smelled so bad that people didn't want to cross it on a bridge has become inviting, a refuge. And, for some, an adventure.

Every ten years or so, Whitbeck and the Merrimack River Watershed Council organize a series of paddling excursions involving dozens of little boats and more than twenty trip leaders. Whitewater experts run the upper reaches of the Pemigewasset and Winnipesaukee and squads of day paddlers (much like our little flotilla on the Concord) make their way down the various tributaries and the main stem of the Merrimack until finally they paddle down the broad tidal estuary sections of the river's main stem, past Newburyport. The trips begin in spring runoff (when high water levels make the whitewater portions of the odyssey possible) and end with a dinner cruise in late summer. A small vial of water collected at Profile Lake in Franconia Notch (the source of the Pemigewasset arm of the Merrimack) is carried all the way down the river, going from the river's highest source to the ocean.

Whitbeck and others organize the big season-long excursion and other, less ambitious trips to help the river by educating those who live and work along its banks.

"It's certainly a much better river than it was ten or fifteen years ago," she told me. "But it's never complete. It's ongoing. And it has to be ongoing."

In other words, the goal keeps moving. And the river keeps getting better and better—more itself. Thoreau would likely have been too much of a loner to take part in the Watershed Council's group activities. But chances are good that he would like the outcome of their work.

Whitbeck and the MRWC are not altruists. Everybody benefits from a cleaner, more beautiful river. And everybody includes them. Gwen and her husband paddle the Merrimack often. "I love being on it," she said. "It's a quiet, beautiful place to be."

But that New Hampshire bluff,—that promontory of a State,—
lowering day and night on this our State of Massachusetts, will
longest haunt our dreams.

—A Walk to Wachusett

4

The Mountains of Home:
Monadnock, Wachusett, Greylock

Though he climbed many other mountains, Henry Thoreau returned most faithfully to Mount Monadnock in southern New Hampshire. Throughout his life, it beckoned to him.

Monadnock's familiar blue shape on the Concord horizon marked the visible outer limit of his everyday world. He could see it clearly from several of the high points around Concord and he remarked on it regularly in his journal. He climbed it four times, beginning in 1844, when he was twenty-seven years old. He climbed it again in 1852, again in 1858, and finally in 1860, just a few months before he contracted his final illness. Each time he went to Monadnock, his trips became more focused and more ambitious. He studied the botany and geology of the mountain more and more carefully with each visit, and camped there longer each time.

He wrote ever-longer journal entries about the mountain and may have been considering writing a book-length study of mountain ecology based on his Monadnock trips. His untimely death in 1862 put an end to that project, and his lengthy and enthusiastic journal entries are now the only record of his observations there. They are still enjoyable to read, and historians consider them among the best 19th-century studies of the mountain. Although he wrote nothing about Monadnock on his first trip, his accounts of his later trips give us a very clear picture of his activities on and around the mountain.

They tell us, for example, that he traveled from Concord to Monadnock on the mass transit of his day—the train. Though Thoreau had decidedly mixed feelings about the railroad, it was the quickest, easiest way to get to Mount Monadnock, so Thoreau used it. After he got off the train at one of the nearby stations, he walked. Most characteristically, he went cross-country in a compass-straight line, directly to the summit.

Even in 1844, steam trains were a new mode of transportation, powerful, noisy, dirty, and fast. They were transforming America, and in New England, they rolled through a countryside that had also been transformed—by agriculture. The landscape through which this new-fangled contraption puffed and rumbled had been vigorously over-farmed, because of the growing nation's demand for wool.

New England's mania for sheep-farming had just peaked in the 1840s, and the landscape, like the sheep, had been sheared—it was eighty percent deforested. Pastures went to the top of good-sized hills and climbed the mountainsides. There wasn't enough wood left for split-rail fencing, so farmers built stone walls to enclose their fields. There was—and still is—plenty of stone.

And so Thoreau rode a clanking, whistling iron horse through a wide-open, semi-barren countryside. He could see for miles.

"Almost without interruption we had the mountain in sight before us," he wrote in 1858. "—its sublime gray mass—that antique, brownish-gray, Ararat color. Probably these crests of the earth are for the most part of one color in all lands, that gray color of antiquity, which nature loves; color of unpainted wood, weather-stain, time-stain; not glaring nor gaudy; the color of all roofs, the color of things that endure, and the color that wears well. . . ."

Once near the mountain, Thoreau's usual practice was to take a compass bearing on the summit (he was a skilled surveyor, familiar with a compass), and then follow that bearing straight toward it, ignoring roads, trails, and whatever obstacles might get in his way. There is a story—probably apocryphal—that once, when he and a companion encountered a farmhouse directly in their path, they walked in the front door, straight through the house, and out the back door, leaving the inhabitants surprised, to say the least.

But perhaps not completely astonished. Monadnock was already in the 1840s and 50s attracting crowds of hikers. Thoreau mentions them several times, grumbles about their litter and graffiti on the summit, and goes to great lengths to avoid them.

The mountain's popularity continues today. In fact, it is overused, and for fairly obvious reasons. It is a dramatic, isolated peak, the largest mountain close to Boston and the other cities of down-country New England, and a relatively easy climb. Its bare summit offers exceptionally wide and sweeping views, from Boston in the southeast to—on a clear day—Mount Washington, one hundred miles to the north. Its Native American name, Monadnock, means literally "the mountain that stands alone." Because it is so perfect an example of the type, geologists now apply the name to all isolated mountains that stand above an eroded plain. And to distinguish it from the rest of the small-m monadnocks, this one is termed the "Grand Monadnock," a fitting distinction.

At only 3,165 feet in elevation, it should be completely forested. (Another monadnock of similar height, Mount Ascutney, forty miles north in Vermont, is wooded to its summit.) But the Grand Monadnock's bare summit is not a completely natural phenomenon. A major hurricane in 1815 toppled and shattered its forests, leaving the mountain swathed in a chaotic mantle of dead and broken trees. In 1820, neighboring farmers decided that the wolves harassing their livestock must have made dens in the impenetrable tangle of fallen trees, and so set fire to it. The resulting blaze completely consumed all the dead wood, along with the live trees, any wolves, and all the forest topsoil of the upper slopes. The mountain was left with a bare cap of rock—which it wears today.

Because it is so dramatically isolated and so identifiable, Mount Monadnock, the Grand Monadnock, has come to define the region it dominates. The dozen or so southwestern New Hampshire towns surrounding it—roughly from Keene in the northwest to Rindge in the south and Peterborough to the east—all focus on the stony peak that towers above them. They are known collectively as the Monadnock Region, and residents of the area seem to share, on some level, an environmental ethic born of their love for the mountain and the lake-studded rural countryside around it. Land protection efforts go back more than a century there and, from the beginning, they have focused on Mount Monadnock.

The area has its share of sprawling suburban ugliness, to be sure. Pizza parlors, video rentals, big-box stores, and all the other manifestations of contemporary suburbia festoon the fringes of Keene and fill several large malls south of town. Rindge and other towns located right on the Massachusetts border are being quietly overtaken by intensive residential development. Even so, most of the area remains beautiful, forested, and quiet.

Like much of the rest of New England, the local economy has endured dramatic ups and downs over the years. The mania for sheep farming and wool production of the first quarter of the 19th century stripped the hills of timber and fattened many a farmer's wallet—for a time. But with the opening of the West, New England's wool-based economy collapsed, the flat, stone-free fields of the Midwest beckoned, and many of New Hampshire's young farmers never came back. All of northern New England entered a long period of decline.

But the distinctive mountain remained, the lakes were still beautiful, and newcomers who valued that beauty began to migrate there. During the latter half of the 19th century, artists, writers, and others eager for a quiet retreat from the fast-growing cities of the day began to buy up the failed farms and move in. The region quietly changed, and the forest gradually returned. Artists' colonies arose in Dublin and Peterborough and, later, an environmental center was established in Hancock that has since protected more than eight thousand acres of environmentally sensitive land. And all the while, Boston grew and its suburbs began to reach into the towns south and east of Mount Monadnock.

The mountain became a New England landmark, an attraction. The dozens of hikers Thoreau had seen in the 1850s became hundreds, then thousands. Every peak and cranny of the mountain was named, a "Halfway House" was built on an appropriate spur, and amateur trail builders established a weblike network of paths, especially on the mountain's south and southwest faces. "Monadnock's slopes probably bear more historic trails, former trails, ruins, and named minor features than any other mountain in New England," notes the Appalachian Mountain Club's *Southern New Hampshire Trail Guide*. Among these features are a Thoreau Trail that Thoreau never walked and "Thoreau's Seat," a rocky outlook upon which he almost certainly never sat.

Today, although the mountain has been protected against development, it is often overwhelmed with people, especially on summer weekends. It has the reputation of being the second most-climbed mountain in the world, after Japan's Mount Fuji, a claim that is almost certainly untrue. (Several million people annually ascend Mount Tai in China.) Nevertheless, Monadnock is one of the world's most-climbed mountains. The AMC guide also notes that on one fine Columbus Day in the 1970s, "it was ascended by throngs estimated at nearly 10,000 people." Monadnock State Park officials currently estimate that between 110,000 and 125,000 people climb to the summit each year.

～ ～ ～

One of my goals in climbing Mount Monadnock was to avoid hordes of people—even people who may have been inspired by Thoreau's prose. So I chose to climb in May, before the summer hiking season, and on a weekday. My companions were my longtime hiking friend Scott Skinner, Thoreau scholar and outdoorsman J. Parker Huber, and his friend Martina Dancing, an art teacher. Parker, who lives in nearby Brattleboro, Vermont, advised that we go up the Marlboro Trail because it is scenic and relatively little used. It ascends the mountain directly from the west.

We caught our first close-up view of the rocky peak as we drove east, past Keene on Route 101. Soon we were nosing past new housing developments and grossly overblown summer McMansions as we sought out the trailhead. Even after making the turn onto Shaker Farm Road, there were clearings bulldozed out of the woods and large, resort-like houses being erected. Parker, who clearly loves the mountain and has climbed it dozens of times, was troubled. "I wish the state park had been able to buy this land," he said. "These are all new."

We rolled along a tiny dirt road where there were more home lots and construction sites, and then the home sites were no more, and the forest closed back in. We had entered the protected lands of the state park. At the trailhead parking lot, there was a Philadelphia vireo singing in the forest canopy overhead, and we walked about half a mile through a quietly murmuring woodland, dappled with spring sunlight, before the serious climbing began. At the bottom of the first steep section, we stopped to admire a couple of clusters of painted trillium. Thoreau's 1858 hike with Harrison Blake, his friend from nearby Worcester, was in spring, like ours, and he mentioned finding painted trilliums also: "three white, lanceolate, waved-edge petals with a purple base," he reported. "This is the handsomest flower of the mountain. . . ."

We climbed over piles of jumbled rock and a series of open ledges, which gave us wider and wider views of the surrounding countryside. Now instead of farm fields and rambling stone walls, it is almost completely forested, and studded with houses set among the trees.

This is a long-settled country. *Yankee Magazine's* Judson Hale noted in an essay in the beautiful book *Where the Mountain Stands Alone* that on a recent climb to the mountain's summit, "as always, we could see the sun reflecting off countless picture windows that face 'the mountain' throughout the Monadnock region. So many of these homes are hidden away in the woods, seldom seen by anyone. But from the summit of our mountain, their whereabouts are revealed." Later in the essay, he notes that his own house has a view of Monadnock. "During clear, sunny afternoons, our picture windows glint and sparkle up there on the summit too."

Hale captures precisely the affection and the feeling of interconnectedness people in the surrounding towns have for "their" mountain. It is a familiar presence to the people who live in the area, a neighbor, an orienting beacon.

We continue our scramble upwards through the increasingly scrubby spruce forest, and after about two hours clamber up a slanted rock face onto the open summit ridge. The trail goes over the false summit of Dublin Peak, then winds among rock outcroppings, dwarf spruce trees, and bright green shoots of mountain ash, inching ever-higher until it reaches the weather-rounded ledges of the summit.

Suddenly we are standing on an immense rocky shiplike prow above a broad green sea far below. The gentle, surrounding hills, the glittering lakes and undulating forest spread off in all directions around us. On clear days, the view extends for more than a hundred miles. Parker tells me that he has seen snowfields glinting on the sides of Mount Washington from this summit on a clear day.

However, the atmosphere today is misty. The White Mountains and Boston's towers are invisible. Nevertheless, I am reminded of Thoreau's comment:

"But that New Hampshire bluff,—that promontory of a State,— lowering day and night on this our State of Massachusetts, will longest haunt our dreams."

We settle for a smaller view, closer at hand. Picking our way down from the summit, a hundred yards or so back the way we came, we find a lunch spot beside a pretty little bog surrounded by cotton grass and flowering rhodora. It has some standing water in the middle and is about fifteen or twenty feet across—just the size of the small bogs that Thoreau described in his journal as being "a feature of the summit."

Over my right shoulder are the twin rounded hummocks of Pack Monadnock and Little Pack Monadnock mountains, and Parker notes that Thoreau referred to them as "the Peterborough Hills," because they are near that village, now invisible in the ubiquitous forest cover. We eat and talk quietly, enjoying the mountaintop for a little while longer.

Then we pack our lunch things away, and make our way down off the stony mountaintop, through the forest, and to the world, waiting for us below. The vireo is still singing when we return to the forested parking lot and open Scott's sun-heated car.

Within a half-hour we are stuck in a steaming traffic jam near the big malls on Route 101. It takes us another twenty minutes or so to work our way around the south edges of Keene, past the malls, which have been built right atop what was once a very nice, extensive marshland.

— — —

From Monadnock's summit, Thoreau could look west and see a series of ranges culminating in the mountain that he knew as Saddleback and that is today called Mount Greylock. At 3,491 feet in elevation, it is the highest point in Massachusetts. Toward the end of his 1860 sojourn on the mountain (he had camped there a week with his friend Ellery Channing, studying the plants and rocks of the mountain), on a clear evening, he counted eight distinct ranges of mountains with Saddleback rising above them, almost mythically high:

"I never saw a mountain that looked so high and so melted away at last cloud-like into the sky, as Saddleback this eve, when your eye had clomb to it by these eight successive terraces," he wrote. "You had to begin at this end and ascend step by step to recognize it for a mountain at all. If you had first rested your eye on it, you would have seen it for a cloud, it was so incredibly high in the sky."

Standing atop the "incredibly high" mountain some 146 years after Thoreau's vision, I tried to locate Monadnock. I puzzled and puzzled over the mountains off to the east. Then finally I asked state ranger Ellis Rud, who was on the mountaintop that day, to help me.

"That's Monadnock," he said pointing northeast. "The big one."

And sure enough, it did look prodigiously big despite its modest height—an immense prow of pale blue stone rising to fill the horizon.

Thoreau had climbed both Monadnock and Greylock on the same

excursion in July 1844. It was one of his first mountain climbing trips, and part of the program of finding himself that he embarked upon after his brother John's death. He also may have had another painful reason to get out of Concord that summer. He and Edward Hoar had accidentally set fire to some valuable Concord woodland just ten weeks earlier, and the town was probably buzzing angrily about it. Whatever his motivations, Thoreau's roundabout process of exploration and self-exploration was a valuable one. It ultimately led him to Walden Pond.

He apparently never wrote anything about his first climb of Monadnock. But he did include a detailed account of his climb up Greylock in *A Week on the Concord and Merrimack Rivers*. It is an interesting account, with moments of self-consciously "Transcendentalist" musings, and other moments of sharply observed realism more characteristic of his later writing style.

He climbed Greylock from the north, along a narrow valley called the Bellows Pipe—a name given because in certain weather conditions, the valley funnels winds along its length and then, near the head of the valley, directs them upward, shooting a stream of mist straight up into the sky like smoke from a factory stack. Ranger Rud tells me that the phenomenon can still be observed—in fact, it is an attraction to youthful hang-gliders who ride the column of mist high into the sky and then glide downward, landing miles away in Massachusetts or Vermont.

When Thoreau walked up it, the valley was open farmland, deforested like most of the rest of New England. At one farmhouse, he encountered an attractive woman and described her vividly:

"Its mistress was a frank and hospitable young woman, who stood before me in a dishabille, busily and unconcernedly combing her long black hair while she talked, giving her head the necessary toss with each sweep of the comb, with lively, sparkling eyes, and full of interest in that lower world from which I had come, talking all the while as familiarly as if she had known me for years, and reminding me of a cousin of mine." Later researchers have surmised that the "frank and hospitable young woman" was probably Rebecca Darling Eddy, wife of a farmer with the wonderful 19th-century name of Preserved Eddy who lived at the head of the valley.

Thoreau (perhaps understandably) thought of spending more time there, but forged on and, following his favorite method, climbed directly to the summit, forsaking the trail. There he camped overnight, huddled against the side of a wooden observation tower built by Williams College students. He covered himself and his blanket with boards as the night chill descended, a mildly bizarre tactic that Thoreau proclaimed quite effective against the cold. Later commentators have noted how similar Thoreau's nest of boards was to a coffin!

He awoke the next morning to find himself above the clouds. In an appropriately Transcendental passage, he declared:

"As the light increased I discovered around me an ocean of mist, which by chance reached up exactly to the base of the tower, and shut out every vestige of the earth, while I was left floating on this fragment of the wreck of a world, on my carved plank in cloudland; a situation which required no aid from the imagination to render it impressive."

Professor William Howarth, in his book *Walking with Thoreau*, notes that this passage is a typical *aubade*—a literary serenade of morning, precisely the sort often found in classical poems. It is also worth noting that the conventional everyday world of lower elevations, which had been causing Thoreau so much grief, was completely masked by the convenient cloudbank. Thoreau was thus able to witness a new world, his slate completely wiped clean of past failures and missteps, "the new terra firma perchance of my future life."

He then proceeded down off the mountain to Pittsfield, where his friend Ellery Channing was waiting to meet him.

— — —

The Bellows Pipe Trail today generally follows Thoreau's route up Greylock. It leads along the same narrow valley, but instead of proceeding through open farmland, the route is now completely forested, and the hiker walks for more than a mile along a woods road. The trail climbs gradually higher, crossing brooks and passing by occasional obscure cellar holes and the ruins of rock walls. Eventually it reaches a lean-to hiking shelter, and at that point begins a steeper climb following a ski trail, which is cleared twenty-five or thirty feet wide in places. There's no ski lift. This trail and the historic Thunderbolt Trail nearby are maintained for backcountry skiers. You have to be hardy enough to climb up the mountain before skiing down.

It's early June when I climb the mountain and the wildflowers of spring are in bloom along the Bellows Pipe Trail: a few yellow blossoms of clintonia (blue-bead lily), lots of Canada mayflower, Canada violet, foamflower (false miterwort), a few late-blooming purple trilliums, and, near the summit, the large white clusters of hobblebush blossoms. The spring greens of the forest are interrupted along several ridges by large brown swaths of trees defoliated by tent caterpillars. But not every creature regards the infestation with displeasure—near the summit, I hear (but do not see) a black-billed cuckoo calling. They regard tent caterpillars as a tasty food source and, as a result of the caterpillar infestation, cuckoos are being seen in numbers all over the Northeast.

The trail crosses the summit road, scrambles up a rocky gully, and emerges in another world: I find myself in a bizarre little summit park, with mown grass lawns, paved pathways, and, on the rounded summit, a weird art deco granite tower, more than ninety feet tall, topped by a glass-and-steel globe that can be electrically illuminated!

It is mildly disorienting to emerge from the forest into what feels vaguely like a city park surrounding a granite lighthouse. The tower is the Massachusetts War Memorial, erected by the state during the Great Depression; it was a public works project that made national news at the time. Locating it here might seem to make it a contender for Bad Idea of the Year (1932), but such is the fate of "highest" mountains. Other, perhaps more appropriate public works projects here are the rustic Bascomb Lodge (1936–38), off to one side of the cleared area, and Thunderbolt Ski Lodge (1940), tucked into the woods just below the summit.

The interior of the tower is dank and gloomy, and the spectacular views from the now-cleared summit seem more pleasant and somehow healthier when viewed from the encircling paved paths. The Hoosic River Valley, the Green Mountains shouldering off into Vermont, and both flat-topped Wachusett and huge, hulking Monadnock, sixty miles off to the northeast, are all visible on a clear day.

Ellis Rud, the helpful summit ranger, shows me a picture of the wooden tower built by Williams College students in 1840. Rud has an interesting interpretation of Thoreau's night amidst the boards. He believes that instead of balancing a board and a rock on himself (as Henry claimed to have done) that Thoreau leaned some of the lumber up against the tower "and then kind of scooted in under it." It's an interesting explanation and certainly makes more sense than Thoreau's own description.

I wander around the summit for a while, taking in the views, and discover that Thoreau's visit is permanently memorialized here. There are rocks with quotations from his account of his climb spotted along the paths. One quotes his above-the-clouds visionary experience while another, in a reference to Williams College—at the base of Greylock in Thoreau's time and ours, notes:

"It were as well to be educated in the shadow of a mountain as in more classical shades. Some will remember, no doubt, not only that they went to the college, but that they went to the mountain."

It is a good thought to ponder, and so I shoulder my backpack and trudge back down the Bellows Pipe.

Mount Wachusett in central Massachusetts is easily the least imposing of the mountains Thoreau climbed. At 2,006 feet in elevation, it is really little more than a large hill, and is almost 1,500 feet lower than either Mount Monadnock or Mount Greylock. Its presence was important to Thoreau, however. He often noted its blue humplike shape on the western horizon, and seemed to feel—or at least to have willed himself to feel—a special kinship with it because it stood alone, off by itself. In an early poem, he wrote:

"But special I remember thee,

Wachusett, who like me

Standest alone without society."

In July of 1842, he walked the twenty-six miles from Concord to Wachusett with Richard Fuller, the younger brother of Margaret Fuller. Margaret, a major Transcendentalist figure, was then editor of the *Dial*, to which Thoreau contributed articles. The two young men walked through the hot July countryside, cooled their feet in the brooks they crossed, lodged overnight at a farmhouse, and then climbed to the bare summit of little Wachusett.

They camped overnight on the summit and then hiked home the following day. Thoreau subsequently wrote an essay in which he inflated the significance of nearly every aspect of the trip. It is written in his most florid early style, replete with classical references and the stock rhetorical flourishes of the Romantic movement. Virgil, Humboldt, Wordsworth, and various mythological references are included, as was the fashion in "literary" writing of the day. Cattle are not cows, but "kine," the two men are pilgrims "under the sign of Jupiter," and when the day grows hot, Thoreau remembers "our fellow traveler, Hassan, in the desert," and quotes some lines from William Collins's *Persian Eclogues*. The landscape is idealized and made pastoral wherever possible.

"Every tinkling sound told of peace and purity," Thoreau wrote, and he noted that the hops being grown around Acton and Bolton "may afford a theme for future poets." Thoreau and Fuller would have passed near or possibly through the mill town of Clinton and, years later in his journal, Thoreau carefully described the working of the textile mill machinery there. But in "A Walk to Wachusett," he does not mention the mills at all. The landscape is depicted as completely, properly pastoral.

The essay was published in *The Boston Miscellany* in January of 1843. It is important to remember that Thoreau was only twenty-five years old when he wrote "A Walk to Wachusett," and he was still learning his craft. Later, his writing would improve dramatically, especially after his two years at Walden Pond, becoming leaner, more factual, and more direct.

Today the territory that Thoreau walked is largely suburban and residential. The region's two big urban areas—Worcester to the south and Leominster to the north—provide most of the wealth that fuels this tidy land. But they keep a proper distance. The little villages cluster around well-kept greens and along streets lined with maples and oaks. Clinton, now a slightly shabby little mercantile city, seems out of sync with the generally pervading air of discreet rural wealth and gentrification. Between Sterling and West Sterling, big oaks and maples arch over Route 140, and stone walls that once bordered farm fields now wander picturesquely through the woods.

Because of the near-universal forest cover, there is no view of Wachusett until you're right on top of it. But then the road swings toward the west and there the mountain is, standing above its little pond, its sides scored with parallel ski trails.

Before driving to the summit, I stop at the state-run visitor center, which has displays on the origin and history of the mountain, and its current flora and fauna. Thoreau is not mentioned in the displays, despite his obvious affection for the mountain and the fact that he climbed it three times. (Twice on his second excursion there, in October of 1854, with his friend Harrison Blake and a visiting Englishman, Thomas Cholmondeley.) On a back wall of the visitor center is a glass-fronted case containing eighty-six different stuffed birds. A few of their live counterparts are singing in the woods outside.

The park runs a variety of nature programs for children and co-sponsors a chili competition, a bicycle race, and other events. In the fall, Wachusett is an important hawk-watching site. As I drive up the summit road, I notice several family groups with children hiking their way upward.

The nearly flat summit is a mishmash of graveled parking lots, Depression-era stone-and-mortar structures, a couple of radio relay stations, and a fenced-off, unused fire tower. Off to one side is a small, stone-rimmed pond populated with schools of small goldfish. The view, however, is impressive, with Mount Monadnock rising dark blue off to the north and the towers of downtown Boston clearly visible, some fifty miles off to the east. The rest of Massachusetts is spread out around the mountain like a giant, blue-and-green mandala.

Thoreau in 1842 called Wachusett "the observatory of the state," and noted that Massachusetts lay spread out beneath him "like a map." He and Fuller camped on the summit, which even then had some development. They camped near the foundations of an abandoned tower. Thoreau claimed to feel "a sense of remoteness, as if we had traveled into distant regions, to Arabia Petraea, or the farthest East." Honesty regarding Wachusett's modest height and gentle summit forced him to admit, "There was little of the sublimity and grandeur which belong to mountain scenery, but an immense landscape to ponder on a summer's day." To maintain the proper Pastoral/Romantic mode, they read Virgil's *Georgics* and Wordsworth's *Peter Bell* in their tent.

They ate a frugal supper of fresh-picked blueberries and milk that they had carried up the mountain (from a nearby farm, perhaps). Late at night, they could see a large fire blazing on Monadnock, "which lighted up the whole western horizon," Thoreau reported. The night was windy and cold, as mountain nights can still be, even in July. The next day, the two young men enjoyed the sunrise, then descended from the mountain and walked home, Fuller to Groton, Thoreau back to Concord.

Camping is now prohibited on the summit of Wachusett and the mountain remains no Arabia Petraea, but a modest and inviting human playground. By all appearances, it is a treasured one. Helmeted bikers in snug, brightly colored costumes pant and pedal up the summit road, and family groups climb the many hiking trails through the forest, looking back for the view as they cross the wide, treeless swaths of the ski trails.

Near the edge of the "Indian Summer" ski trail, a careful observer can find a clean-cut, square cellar hole. This is all that remains of the two-hundred-acre farm that John Roper established here in 1792. Roper was a Revolutionary War veteran who bought land and built a farmhouse in preparation for his marriage to young Dorcas Kilburn. We know the Roper farm must have existed when Thoreau walked to Wachusett (although he doesn't mention it) because the farm was visited in 1860 by the poet John Greenleaf Whittier, who mentioned it obliquely in his poem "Monadnock from Wachusett."

Most of those who pass by the farm site today—skiers in winter, hikers and bikers in summer—have no inkling of the quiet human dramas played out on the mountain's flanks two centuries ago.

Wachusett is still beloved by the people of Massachusetts. As I wander around the summit, I fall into conversation with Steve Cloutier of nearby Townsend, who has been climbing the mountain regularly for fifty years—ever since he was two! With him is his fifteen-year-old son, Michael, who wears a T-shirt that proclaims, "May the Forest Be With You!"

Steve and Michael climb the mountain in summer and ski it in winter. Today they are pleased with their effort: they made it up the Old Indian Trail in thirty-five minutes. Neither of them seems at all tired, not even winded. An elderly man in a porkpie hat approaches them and raps with his cane on the stone parapet upon which they are sitting. "Know who built that?" he asks. "The C.C.C." He adds with a smile: "Take care of it . . . a lot of somebody's work went into that!" The elderly gent and his family wander off to another Civilian Conservation Corps–built parapet and sit looking off at the view. A family of hikers, each bearing a wooden staff, emerges from the woods below and trudges to the summit.

Steve tells me that the champion hiker in his family has to be his mother, Pauline Cloutier, now in her seventies. She has climbed Wachusett more than a thousand times.

Of the three mountains close to Concord that Thoreau climbed, only Monadnock has been left completely wild—undeveloped, unpaved, un-bedecked with observation towers, memorial towers, communications towers—in a word, unspoiled. Paved roads lead to the summits of both Wachusett and Greylock. Only hiking trails go to the rocky summit of Monadnock. This is because the people who live around that mountain love it and have passionately defended it against development for almost a century.

Abbott Thayer, one of the artists who immigrated to the region in the late 1800s, was the first to publicly sound the call for the mountain's protection. Thayer, whose paintings depicted Monadnock as an incandescent presence, glowing powerfully above the dark surrounding hills, was horrified when he encountered new houses and no-trespassing signs on its flanks on one of his hikes. Such things, he declared, were a blot on the mountain's "primeval wild nature-purity." Monadnock belonged to everyone, he declared. It must never be developed. "Those spruces, after all the centuries of hermit and olive-backed thrush voices," he declared, "shall not know the Victor talking machine if I can stop it."

Thayer, who appears to have been considered as much a pain in the neck as his predecessor Henry David Thoreau, enlisted the aid of the Society for the Protection of New Hampshire Forests in the cause. And in 1913, the society was able to acquire 406 crucial acres that ringed the summit—the summit itself previously having been conserved by the town of Jaffrey. The society pledged "to maintain forever its wild and primeval conditions, where the forest and rock shall remain undisturbed in their wild state, where birds and game shall find their natural refuge."

There was a stone fire tower atop the mountain from 1928 through 1969, but it was eventually taken down. In 1944, a Keene radio station announced its plans to build a transmitting tower there and a tramway to the summit. Opponents fought the idea, and eventually obtained an option on the old Halfway House property, effectively killing the proposal. In 1987, Monadnock was named a National Natural Landmark and that designation, combined with the strong advocacy of the Society for the Protection of New Hampshire Forests, appears likely to keep the mountain itself free from development forever.

Since then the society has continued to acquire land on and around the mountain, eventually protecting one of the largest conserved landscapes in New England. Of the 6,817 conserved acres on Mount Monadnock, the organization owns more than half, plus additional acreage on nearby Gap Mountain. The Harris Center for Conservation Education in nearby Hancock has conserved some 8,800 additional acres of environmentally sensitive land in the region.

Like most of New England, the Monadnock region is threatened by development pressure. New Hampshire is one of the fastest growing states in the nation, and much of that growth is being fueled by suburban expansion from the Boston metropolitan region. Towns like Rindge, close to the Massachusetts border, fear losing their small-town identity in the continuing rush of home building. Between 1950 and 2000, the population of Rindge mushroomed from 707 to 5,451, an increase of 670 percent. New big-box stores and the big shopping centers (and resulting traffic jams) south of Keene are further evidence of the pressures facing the region.

The Grand Monadnock rises above the tamed, pleasant landscape of southwestern New Hampshire, a relic reminder of an ancient, less-tamed past. The mountain has been protected against development; the landscape surrounding it has not. And so the region around Monadnock is in flux.

The area is no longer pastoral. Farming has all but disappeared, and most of the farm fields have gone back to forest. Yet there is a feeling that mankind and nature are integrated here, living in harmony. And that feeling has overtones and echoes of pastoralism. Hiking trails cruise the undeveloped, woodsy places and climb the modest hills surrounding Mount Monadnock. There are easy walks to scenic ledges, hilltops, ponds, and bogs. It is an exceptionally pleasant place, forested hills interspersed with lakes and small villages. Nature seems to be accepted on its own terms, woven into the fabric of human life, a gentle, much-appreciated presence.

New England's wilder, more rugged places are an exciting amplification of this gentler version of nature. On the cover of the Appalachian Mountain Club's *Southern New Hampshire Trail Guide* is a photograph of a young father, hiking with his small son in a backpack carrier. They are taking in the view of an island-studded lake from an open rock ledge above it. It's a very different image from the great soaring peaks and heroic hikers used by guidebooks to depict the wilder mountains of the north. It's a perfect illustration of a feeling that the Monadnock Region creates—that this would be a nice place to introduce children to the wonders of nature.

You wouldn't want this tamer landscape to be New England's only expression of nature. But it is a reassuring vision, nonetheless, of what a settled countryside can be.

One only hopes that the balance so well expressed here can be maintained.

I looked with awe at the ground I trod on.... This was that Earth of which we have heard, made out of Chaos and Old Night. Here was no man's garden, but the unhandselled globe. It was not lawn, nor pasture, nor mead, nor woodland, nor lea, nor arable, nor waste land. It was the fresh and natural surface of the planet Earth, as it was made, forever and ever....

— The Maine Woods

5

Katahdin: Greatest Mountain

Good news: the sky is clear!" Michael reported as I crawled out of my sleeping bag at 5:30 AM.

That was good news indeed. The thunderstorms of the night before seemed to be over. The only clouds we could see hovered at the top of the mountain. Surely they would burn off by the time we got to timberline.

The day was already humid—close and muggy—even though the temperature was only in the 70s. I felt foolish as I packed a wool hat and fleece sweater along with my rain jacket. But there was the possibility of thundershowers in the forecast and Katahdin is a known weather-breeder with a huge area of bare rock above treeline. So all the extra clothing went in along with extra food and two full liters of water.

We were walking up the Abol Trail before 8 AM. Our early start was another precaution, because we guessed that if thunderstorms did come, they'd come late in the day. That was the way it had happened yesterday, the way it often happens in the mountains. But we were not expecting storms. The sky, after all, was almost entirely clear.

After an hour in the woods, we reached the bottom of the Abol Slide and began climbing upward, over rocks and boulders. The higher we climbed, the more we could see of the immense forest that extended outward, beyond and beneath us.

My thoughts turned to Henry Thoreau and his attempt to climb this mountain in 1846. Though I had been to Katahdin several times before, he was my current reason for making this climb by this route.

In my search for Thoreau—or perhaps more accurately, echoes of Thoreau, resonances of Thoreau—I traveled to the parts of New England he visited and wrote about. Katahdin, in north-central Maine, is one of those places, an essential and important one.

That is because Katahdin (or "Ktaadn," as Thoreau spelled it) changed the way the great New England author thought about nature. His experience on the mountain helped ground his airy Transcendentalism in reality, and lodged in his heart a lasting affection for the North Woods of Maine. From his account of his climb in *The Maine Woods*, it is clear that the mountain fascinated and enchanted him.

He climbed it once, in September of 1846. And he dreamt about the mountain, sleeping and awake, for the rest of his life.

When Thoreau came to Katahdin in 1846, only a handful of people had actually climbed the mountain, and there were no trails. However, Abol Slide, which makes a clear and obvious route to the mountain's broad summit plateau, had fallen in 1816, thirty years before he arrived. Others had ascended the mountain by that route. Thoreau chose not to.

It was not a good decision. It would involve Thoreau in a lot of very rugged bushwhacking—and would ultimately keep him from the summit.

He made his decision partly because of his own stubborn nature, and partly because of the nature of his trip. In 1846, Thoreau was in the second summer of his great social experiment of one—living in his cabin on the shore of Walden Pond. He had identified the central concern of his relatively short life—forging an understanding of his relationship with nature. In Concord and at Walden Pond nature was gentle, fecund, and benign. But Thoreau, the Romantic, wanted sterner stuff. He came to Maine seeking wildness, the force that he believed controls and drives the universe.

Today, the drive from Bangor, up the interstate to Millinocket and from there to Baxter State Park, takes a couple of hours. Thoreau had to battle upriver by bateau for three full days just to reach the base of the mountain. In his first view of Katahdin, even though its heights were partially obscured with clouds, he saw it as portentous, a "dark isthmus . . . connecting the heavens with the earth."

His excitement grew as he got closer: "We were about to float over unmeasured zones of earth," he wrote as he approached Katahdin, "bound on unimaginable adventures."

He was to get the North Woods adventure he sought—perhaps even more than he had bargained for. And so, on a much smaller scale, was I.

—— ⋯ ——

K ette Adene," the Native Americans called it: "Greatest Mountain." Very few who have seen it or climbed it would disagree, even today. Katahdin remains the Northeast's wildest, most exciting mountain, a mountain with a distinctive presence.

Yet it is also, in its subtle New England way, a trickster mountain, a shape-shifter.

Several of the White Mountains in New Hampshire are higher; Mount Washington stands more than a thousand feet above its Maine neighbor. But the summit of Mount Washington is a commercial travesty: parking lots, a cog railway station that unloads tourists by the score, steps and railings, lots of pavement, and a summit building selling souvenirs and hot dogs. Katahdin is crossed only by foot trails.

Many other New England peaks are huge, wild, and wonderful. But Katahdin is all that and more. Call it style: the rocky drama of its enormous cliffs, the rounded peaks and saw-toothed Knife Edge, a feeling of wilderness that is palpable. Most of all Katahdin is mysterious, a mile-high crumpled mass of stone that appears dramatically different when seen from different angles. It refuses to be defined.

From the south, the direction it is usually approached from,

Katahdin presents a familiar face: a rising forested wall, almost tentlike in form, capped by a gentle stone peak. This is the familiar view, the view on uncounted thousands of T-shirts and paintings and baseball caps and posters. From this viewpoint, the mountain looks deceptively simple: a mountain, a peak.

But here the mystery begins—because from many southern vantage points, the actual summit of the mountain cannot be seen at all. Its front buttress looks like the highest peak but is not. South Peak, which is visible, is not quite as high as the more reclusive Baxter Peak. The closer you get to the mountain from the south, the less likely you are to see the actual summit.

From other directions, the mountain presents other faces.

Seen from the east, Katahdin breaks into a range of scattered summits and a raw, saw-toothed ridge: the famed "Knife Edge," arguably the most exciting hiking trail in the East. At the end of the Knife Edge stands a conical peak named Pamola, after the angry Native American deity said to guard the mountain jealously. It is a beautiful symmetrical eminence, but not one of the highest points on the range.

From some eastern angles, Katahdin looks like a giant loaf, carved up by a rough-edged knife, or like a sleeping giant, recumbent across the landscape, a humongous knee cast up here, a shoulder shifted there. Its component peaks sprawl across the great Maine forest, subsiding into the northern reaches of Baxter State Park in a vast complex of lakes and trails, forests, swamps, and other, smaller bare stone mountains.

From the west, Katahdin presents itself not as random scattered peaks sliced apart by glaciers, but as a great, elongated, single-bodied mountain massif, a green dragon rearing its stone-capped head to the south and curling into cliffs and rocky tarns to the north. The dragon's head—Baxter Peak, at 5,267 feet in elevation the highest point in Maine—can be seen clearly and is backed by a ragged crest of black stone: the Knife Edge again, just visible over the shoulder of Hamlin Peak. Late in the afternoon, with the sun on its flanks, the mountain glows with power.

Overall, the range is shaped like a huge fish hook with Pamola at the point of the hook, Baxter Peak at the bottom of the curve, and South Peak and the Knife Edge in between. The shaft of the "hook" extends to the north and encompasses Hamlin Peak and the North Peaks as it tails off towards Russell Pond and Grand Lake Matagamon. The hook's inside curve was cored by a hanging glacier. There, in the Great Basin or on Hamlin Ridge, a hiker finds himself suddenly in the Rockies, a realm of two-thousand-foot cliffs, soaring ridges, rock-filled gullies, and giant slides. The mountain almost completely surrounds you and radiant granite energy permeates the air.

And so Katahdin is a mountain with a hundred faces and a thousand moods. The mountain is elusive, a mystery incarnate—or instoneate. It has been mystifying and enchanting hikers and explorers like Henry David Thoreau for many years.

—— — —

The 1846 trip to Katahdin was Thoreau's first visit to Maine. He had left his tiny cabin at Walden Pond, where he was living and writing at the time, and had gone in search of wildness. He brought with him a bateau-load of Romantic assumptions about the Northern Forest, along with his "stout old shoes" and "light India-rubber coat." His move to Walden Pond was both a withdrawal from and a critique of workaday, commercial society, and Thoreau continued that withdrawal and critique in Maine.

Passing lumber mills north of Bangor, he immediately thought of the living trees, majestic and pristine before they were cut down, that had been fed to the mill.

"Think how stood the white-pine tree on the shore of Chesuncook, its branches soughing with the four winds, and every individual needle trembling in the sunlight," he wrote in *The Maine Woods*. "Think how it stands with it now—sold, perchance to the New England Friction-Match Company."

Thus, Thoreau saw the tree literally reduced to splinters, made inconsequential by the commercial, civilized world. Likewise, trade and conformity had leached the romance out of the Penobscot Indians whom Thoreau saw when he went to their village of Old Town in search of a guide. The Indians he met were "dull and greasy-looking," the houses shabby and apparently deserted, with a prosperous church nearby. "These were once a powerful tribe," he wrote, adding, almost in disbelief, "Politics are all the rage with them now."

It would be better, Thoreau declared with sarcastic hyperbole, to see "a row of wigwams, with a dance of pow-wows, and a prisoner tortured at the stake." At the very least, it would better fit his own preconceptions. Over the coming eleven years, Thoreau would temper his Romantic views of what Native Americans should be. And the mountain ahead of him would temper his views of nature.

As he proceeded upriver, away from Bangor and conventional society, the more spare and primitive life became, the more Thoreau liked it.

As soon as he entered the woods (symbolically, by stepping over a fence and leaving the road for a trail), things immediately began to improve. His prose lightened and beautiful images returned. Thoreau even became, in his own vision, a kind of idealized Indian.

"The evergreen woods had a decidedly sweet and bracing fragrance; the air was a sort of diet-drink, and we walked on buoyantly in Indian file, stretching our legs." At "Uncle George" McCauslin's farm, where he stayed two nights on his journey north, Thoreau declared, "The deeper you penetrate into the woods, the more intelligent, and, in one sense, less countrified do you find the inhabitants."

He liked McCauslin, declared him witty and shrewd, and convinced him to come along with him to the mountain. He could not resist the opportunity for yet another jab at his Concord neighbors: "If I were to look for a narrow, uninformed, and countrified mind," he wrote, "it would be among the rusty inhabitants of an old-settled country . . . in the towns about Boston, even on the high road in Concord, and not in the backwoods of Maine."

Approaching Katahdin, Thoreau was enchanted by the beauty of the woods and lakes surrounding the mountain. Even though his feet were constantly wet and his clothing damp from the wet countryside and intermittent rain, he was a man clearly invigorated by the wilderness. The wild solitude pleased him: "No face welcomed us but the fine fantastic sprays of free and happy evergreen trees, waving one above another in their ancient home," he wrote, describing an evening paddle across North Twin Lake.

He reported several moments of transcendent beauty as he approached Katahdin. On September 6, as his party camped on the West Branch of the Penobscot near the mouth of Abol and Katahdin streams, Thoreau described an idyllic interlude of trout fishing in the clear river, with the majestic bulk of Katahdin as a backdrop. The fish were biting, and the group caught them by the dozens. They flung them onto the river shore where Thoreau, who had lost his hook, gathered them up for dinner. The trout seemed celestial, mythological, to him.

"While yet alive, before their tints had faded, they glistened like the fairest flowers, the product of primitive rivers," Thoreau wrote, "and he could hardly trust his senses, as he stood over them, that these jewels should have swum away in that Aboljacknagesic for so long, so many dark ages,—these bright, fluviatile flowers, seen of Indians only, made beautiful, the Lord only knows why, to swim there!"

That night he dreamt of trout fishing and, awakening before dawn, he was unsure whether or not he had dreamed the entire episode. So he arose while his companions were still asleep, baited his hook again, and caught several more trout. The dream was real, he discovered, and the trout as he caught them and swung them to shore "sped swiftly through the moonlight air, describing bright arcs on the dark side of Ktaadn. . . ."

The next morning, with his companions, Thoreau began his epic climb of the mountain. Since their Indian guides had failed to show up, Thoreau himself took charge. "Here it fell to my lot," he wrote, "as the oldest mountain-climber, to take the lead." He was twenty-nine years old.

He decided not to follow the obvious route by which the mountain previously had been climbed—the recent Abol Slide (still a popular hiking route). Instead, he chose his favorite method of bushwhacking toward his goal.

"We determined to steer directly for the base of the highest peak," Thoreau wrote in his account of the adventure in *The Maine Woods*, "leaving a large slide, by which, as I have since learned, some of our predecessors ascended, on our left."

That was Thoreau, marching to his different drummer. The absence of trails suited him just fine; he didn't much like trails anyway.

His preferred method of climbing a mountain was to set off cross-country through the forest, guiding himself by the lay of the land and his compass. He was skilled in compass use because of his sometime occupation as a surveyor. And he was, perhaps obviously, a man who liked to go his own way. He had climbed other New England peaks by simply taking a compass bearing on the summit and following it.

That worked well enough on smaller, less complex mountains like Mount Wachusett, near his home. But when Thoreau tried the same approach on immense, sprawling Katahdin, it proved his undoing.

Part of the reason for his failure to reach the summit was the weather, which wrapped the heights of the mountain in fog. But a greater reason was his own tactical error: Thoreau had set his sights, and his compass, on South Peak, the second-highest point on the mountain.

South Peak, remember, appears to be the highest point on the mountain and is the only real peak you can see from where Thoreau took his compass reading. From that position Baxter Peak, the true summit, is hidden from view.

And so he battled onward through the forest, aiming for the wrong peak. Did his five companions ever look wistfully toward the open rocks of Abol Slide while crashing through the near-impenetrable undergrowth, and blowdowns? No matter.

"Setting the compass for a north-east course, which was the bearing of the southern base of the highest peak, we were soon buried in the woods," Thoreau wrote happily. "It was the worst kind of traveling."

He estimated he traveled fourteen miles through the woods that day. The actual distance is less than four miles.

After hours in the dense, shaggy undergrowth, the party finally made camp below treeline, probably somewhere near the spur today called Rum Mountain. They camped near Abol Stream and Thoreau set out to scramble up the mountain before dark. He clambered up the streambed, got close to treeline, and began walking along the intertwined tops of the krummholz—the dwarfed spruce and fir trees.

"Once, slumping through, I looked down ten feet, into a dark and cavernous region. . . . These holes were bears' dens, and the bears were even then at home."

Well, maybe. One wonders if Thoreau had been imbibing something more potent than arborvitae tea!

He climbed still farther, but was stopped by steep rocks and mist, and returned to his camp for the night.

The next day, he tried again, scrambling over aggregations of loose rock, aiming again at South Peak. He soon climbed ahead of his companions, and clambered upwards toward what he thought was the summit, "still edging toward the clouds,—for though the day was clear elsewhere, the summit was concealed by mist."

This time, Thoreau reached a ridgetop—most likely the ridge connecting Baxter Peak with South Peak—but because of the heavy summit cloud cover he could not tell where the peak he sought might be.

"It was like sitting in a chimney and waiting for the smoke to blow away," he wrote. "It was, in fact, a cloud-factory."

As Thoreau sat alone in a vast wilderness, separated from his companions, somewhat disoriented by the stubborn summit mist, his reactions were interesting and important. First his literary training and impulses asserted themselves, and he thought of "the creations of the old epic and dramatic poets, of Atlas, Vulcan, the Cyclops, and Prometheus." But then he felt frightened and diminished. Even his reason seemed to desert him on the heights: "Some part of the beholder, even some vital part, seems to escape through the loose grating of his ribs as he ascends," he admitted. "He is more lone than you can imagine."

Nature had previously been a friendly, reassuring presence to Thoreau, as it was to other Transcendentalists and Romantics. (Wordsworth had commented fatuously: "Nature never did betray the heart that loved her.") But near the top of Katahdin, Thoreau saw another aspect of nature.

"She does not smile on him as in the plains," he wrote. "She seems to say sternly, why came ye here before your time? . . . Is it not enough that I smile in the valleys? I have never made this soil for thy feet, this air for thy breathing, these rocks for thy neighbors."

Later, less rhetorically, Thoreau wrote simply: "Nature was here something savage and awful, though beautiful. . . . There was there felt the presence of a force not bound to be kind to man."

Nature was no longer a Romantically benign force in harmony with mankind. Now, Thoreau saw, it could be brutally (if majestically) indifferent.

He gave up and clambered back down over the rocks to join his companions, catching, as he descended, some views of the vast complex of woods and lakes that is northern Maine.

Yet, as he descended, a further experience awaited him.

＊＊＊

By the time Michael and I reached the top of Abol Slide, I could understand completely why the mist and clouds stymied Thoreau. We were suddenly in the clouds, too. Even with a trail marked by cairns and paint blazes, it was disorienting. There were no marked trails on the mountain in 1846. (Not that Thoreau would have used them. He turned away from the slide, after all, and that was the closest thing to a clear pathway at that time.) He was on a wild, untracked peak that had been climbed only a few times and about which very little was known.

We had the benefit of signs and clearly marked trails and so had little difficulty making our way to the top of Baxter Peak. As it did with Thoreau, the mist occasionally lifted as we climbed higher, revealing the tawny sedges and rushes growing on the high plateau. It never cleared, however.

We tagged the sign marking the northern terminus of the Appalachian Trail and settled down on an accommodating rock to eat our lunch. However, as we were eating, completely socked in by the blowing mist, Michael said quietly, "I'm going to pretend I didn't hear that thunder. . . ."

A moment later, I heard it, too—a low growling rumble.

"Let's get the hell out of here," I said, as calmly as possible, and we quickly packed up and moved out.

But before we had gone two hundred yards back down the trail, the rain began: first scattered drops, then a steady patter, the cold, harsh winds, and a downpour.

"Dammit," I said, zipping up my rain jacket and toggling down the hood. "Dammit!"

Fortunately, there was no lightning. But the low growls of thunder continued off and on, and the rain increased in intensity. As we made our way down off the peak, we were passed, unbelievably, by people still slogging uphill, determined to make the summit despite the deepening storm.

A young couple bounded down past us without any rain gear—or, apparently, brains. The woman, young, slender, maybe in her twenties, was clad only in formfitting Lycra shorts and a tank top.

"Yes, we're crazy," she giggled as she ran past me, downhill. "Boy, it's cold up here!"

Right. And wet: perfect hypothermia weather. I wondered if we'd find her crumpled beside the trail, dazed and hypothermic or injured. Fortunately we didn't.

Then, the ultimate absurdity—loping upward over the wet stone steps and blocks came a tall, muscular lad wearing sneakers, shorts, an enormous, soggy leather hat—and no shirt! No pack either—i.e., no rain gear, no extra food.

Hypothermia on a stick! Hypothermia waiting to happen. (And in fact, we learned later, he did become hypothermic later on. Fortunately another member of his party happened to have an extra sweater. I still wonder if the stringbean in a hat knows how close he came to dying that day.)

Katahdin is probably at least as dangerous a mountain as Mount Washington. The AMC *Maine Mountain Guide* notes that the weather is similar and that the longer access routes and lack of any summit shelter have contributed to many hiker injuries and several deaths in recent years. There is, in fact, on any large mountain, plenty of opportunity to experience "the presence of a force not bound to be kind to man."

Back at the trail junction in the pouring rain, Michael and I quickly decided not to go down the way we had come up—Abol Slide is not recommended for descent in bad weather. The rain was hard and steady now and the wind seemed to be picking up. We headed down the Hunt Trail (the Appalachian Trail) which is supposed to be safer in a storm. It is, however, a mile longer than the Abol Slide trail, it comes off the mountain three miles from our campsite, and it is, as we would have ample opportunity to experience, a very tough trail.

Fortunately, Michael and I were well prepared. I no longer felt at all foolish about the wool hat I had packed that morning—in the cold, blowing rain, I was wearing it, and glad to have it.

We picked our way westward across the rain-swept plateau, which I could see was narrowing into a slender spur. When I reached the end of the spur, I immediately received two unpleasant surprises.

Wham! A roaring wind slammed into me, almost blowing me off

my feet. The rain, which had been merely wet and cold before, had become icy and stinging. And horizontal, not vertical. Each drop stung like a tiny whiplash. Was there hail in it? Probably not; I didn't see any on the ground. But it felt like there must be, it lashed my face and eyes so.

At the same time, I involuntarily looked down. Damn!

A bare stone ridge dropped steeply away in front of me, a near-vertical stack of pinkish boulders that went down as far as I could see. It was narrow, completely bare and rocky, and looked more like a cliff edge than a trail. At least a thousand feet of steep, wet rocks confronted us.

Individual white streaks of rain slashed in front of me. As if to underline our predicament, a super-gust of wind picked me up and dumped me, gasping, on the rocks. I scrambled to my feet just as Michael arrived at the top of the spur. He crouched as the wind blasted him. "Stay low!" he shouted.

No problem. I had no desire whatsoever to stand erect.

The ridge we had to descend was extremely narrow at its top. A thirty- to forty-foot cliff established its left-hand side, directly ahead of me.

"You must not fall," I told myself. "You can crawl if you need to, but you must not allow yourself to be blown off this ridge. Stay away from that edge."

I crawled across the exposed ridge on hands and knees, then stepped down into a sheltered depression in the rocks. My hiking poles were dangling from the straps around my wrist. They were worse than useless here—the going was just too steep—so I stowed them in my pack and we continued our clumsy, halting descent down the windy ridge.

We squeezed backward through the "Gateway," a narrow space between two granite boulders, and worked our way step-by-step down the steepest part of the ridge. The howling wind blew me off my feet once again, but only my pride was injured—and I didn't have much of that left anyway!

As we reached the bottom of the storm cloud, the gray opaqueness around us began to disappear and vast distances slowly opened up.

Suddenly I was staring into a raging wilderness. An immense vision of rockbound, steep-sided Gothic peaks appeared below me, extending off to the north. The Owl, a striking, pointy-topped plug of granite, reared up far beneath my boots with the Klondike, a bright-green valley swamp, behind it. Still farther off, Barren Peak, Coe, South Brother, and North Brother rose in grey-green ranks, with the huge cliff-bound west flank of Katahdin dwarfing them.

Dark clouds, shot through with white, and sheets of rain raced toward me; wisps of smoky mist were ripped from the vast forest and swirled upward. Torn shreds of blue sky and racing clouds intermingled with shafts of sunlight, even as the roaring winds continued to pummel us, adding to the awesome wild beauty sprawled for miles around.

It was a vision of raw wildness that Thoreau himself would have savored. It was humbling, frightening, savage, uncaring. And completely beautiful.

I instantly knew it was the point of the route we had been forced onto, and of the day itself. I was being granted a vision of that very wildness that Thoreau had come to this mountain seeking. I was suddenly grateful, deeply moved. I said a few words in gratitude. And watched carefully where I placed my next bootstep.

We continued picking our way down the ridge, battling the wind. Younger, stronger hikers passed us: we watched one young couple battle their way, hunched and staggering as they crossed an exposed, wind-swept ridge below us, then followed their example, crouched and struggling across ourselves.

After more than two hours of this, I began to tire and look for the shelter of treeline and easier walking. I reached into my jacket pocket for my glasses, which I had removed high on the mountain, fearing they would be blown away. Nothing!

Damn! "Michael!" I yelled. "I've lost my glasses. I'll have to go back and find them!"

"Tom!" he shouted. "They're on your face!"

I had put them back on a few minutes before and forgotten them.

We continued downward into the trees, laughing. But the episode was sobering—clear evidence that my mind as well as my body was becoming fatigued.

We were soon below treeline, in the protective shelter of the forest once again. And when we emerged at Katahdin Stream Campground after a long slog down the winding trail, we looked back at Katahdin's summit. It was completely clear! No clouds, no storm. But my aching body and soaking boots reassured me that the storm had been real enough.

Fortunately, the first car we thumbed on the park's perimeter road stopped and mercifully gave us a ride back to our campsite on Abol Stream.

— — —

As Thoreau and his friends descended the mountain, they followed the streambed at first, splashing down alongside and through it.

After more orienteering through the forest, they emerged into a large open meadowlike area known as the "burned lands." And here, as never before, Thoreau was suddenly struck with the wonder and strangeness of nature.

"Perhaps I most fully realized that this was primeval, untamed, and forever untameable *Nature*, or whatever else men call it, while coming down this part of the mountain," he wrote. In a passage that builds in intensity, he declares that he looked with awe at the earth he trod on and even his own body. His writing becomes peppered with exclamation points and italics. It is excited, gasping, verging on incomprehensibility:

"Talk of mysteries!—Think of our life in nature," he declares, "daily to be shown matter, to come in contact with it—rocks, trees, wind on our cheeks! the *solid* earth! the *actual* world! the *common sense*! *Contact*! *Contact*! *Who* are we? *where* are we?"

Something clearly happened to Thoreau. There is no other passage in *The Maine Woods*, *Walden*, or anywhere in any of his other books even remotely similar to this ecstatic outburst.

David M. Robinson, in his book *Natural Life*, suggests that Thoreau had what amounts to an enlightenment experience, "a profound and mysterious encounter with the sources of being."

A friend of mine had a simpler explanation: "Thoreau went nuts up there, you know," he said.

Whatever happened to Thoreau, it passed quickly. His narrative returns to calmness as he and his companions make their two-day journey back to Bangor and 19th-century American civilization.

But his view of nature was changed. His understanding became more complex, less Romantic, and much more based in observable facts.

Thoreau's Katahdin experience, it would seem, shook him to the soles of his boots. The mountain, as it does with so many who visit it, penetrated deeply into his heart. Years later, in a letter to a friend, he wrote of Katahdin:

"I keep a mountain anchored off eastward a little way, which I ascend in my dreams both awake and asleep."

And more years later, as he lay slowly dying, Thoreau's last, semiconscious words suggested that he had returned once more, in his dreams, to the wilderness of northern Maine.

"Moose," he muttered feverishly, ". . . Indians. . . . "

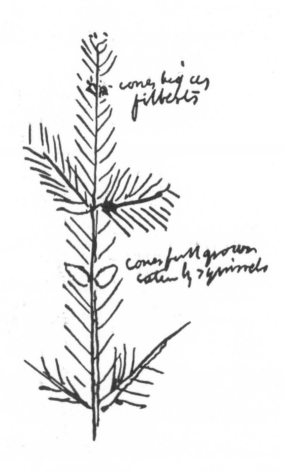

Pine bough and cones, sketch from Thoreau's journal, January 22, 1856

There are not only stately pines, but fragile flowers, like the orchises, commonly described as too delicate for cultivation, which derive their nutriment from the crudest masses of peat. These remind us, that not only for strength, but for beauty, the poet must, from time to time, travel the logger's path and the Indian's trail, to drink at some new and more bracing fountain of the Muses, far in the recesses of the wilderness.

—The Maine Woods

6

Northern Maine: Big Woods, Big Question

In far-northern Maine, north of Bangor, north of Greenville and Millinocket, lie the vast forests that entranced Henry David Thoreau. Although the region is no longer a true wilderness, it is wild enough. It is the largest officially uninhabited area in the continental United States—roughly ten million acres of woods and lakes, mountains and rivers, penetrated only by primitive logging roads.

A scattering of people live in the region year-round. And the great forest has been logged repeatedly and hard—brutally hard in some places. Stands of big, old-growth trees are now unusual. Huge clear-cuts scar the region.

But when you go to northern Maine, you know you're not in Kansas anymore. It still feels as wild as anyplace in North America.

Unbroken forests line the shores of Chesuncook and Chamberlain lakes and there's hardly a campsite, let alone a cabin, for miles. At times you feel as though you've dropped off the edge of the map.

The region is a great, soggy plateau. The headwaters of Maine's greatest rivers—the Kennebeck, the Penobscot, the Allegash, and the St. John—rise there, dissecting it into a chaos of valleys, rivers, and lakes. Out of the midst of this immense lake-studded highland rises Katahdin, Maine's tallest peak, surrounded by smaller attendant mountains: Doubletop, North and South Brother, the Traveler. Other mountains lift their stony shoulders out of the surrounding forest. It is an incomparable wild complex of lakes and streams and peaks.

And hanging over this big country is an almost equally big question: what is the future of the Maine woods? What will happen to this great wild place?

Henry David Thoreau asked the same question 150 years ago. It is still being asked, and for a very good reason. The Maine woods is New England's last deep wilderness, one of the last in the United States. The struggle for its future is more than just a state matter: it has both regional and national significance.

When Thoreau first came to Bangor in 1838, looking for a teaching job, he met "an old Indian" who planted the seed of his fascination with the Maine woods. "Two or three mile up the river one beautiful country," he told Thoreau. Even though the Maine woods have been changed enormously since then, weakened and exploited in many ways, the characterization still holds true. It is still "one beautiful country."

For Thoreau, it was more than beautiful. It was the abode of the wildness he sought, and it refreshed and inspired him every time he went there. He traveled to northern Maine three times—in 1846, 1853, and 1857. Each time he learned more about the place and became more familiar with the Native Americans who called it home.

He climbed Katahdin—not quite to the summit—on his first trip in 1846, and never again. Though he wanted to and expected to, it never worked out. But he did plunge deeply into the Maine woods. His 1857 trip, especially, was a major excursion, a bold foray into the heart of Maine's wildest country that took him completely around Katahdin, through several of Maine's largest lakes, and down untamed sections of both the West Branch and East Branch of the Penobscot River.

Bangor was then a logging town and the last outpost of 19th-century urbanity. Thoreau began both of his latter trips by taking the stagecoach from there to Greenville at the southern end of Moosehead Lake.

In the 1850s, Greenville was a small logging village. Today, it is a small tourist village, complete with inns and restaurants of all levels of price and pretentiousness, gift shops, a good local library, banks, an eclectic outdoor outfitter's shop with good coffee and Internet access, and, a few hundred yards away, a friendly sports bar that calls itself "The Stress-Free Moose."

As you drive north to Greenville, farm fields give way to forest, and the road assumes the classic Maine configuration, going arrow-straight through the swamps and forest for a half-mile or so, disappearing as it climbs over a low, wooded hill, up and over that hill, and onto another long straight stretch of empty road that, in turn, disappears over the next low, shaggy rise. As you go farther north, you see more flashing yellow-lighted signs, warning of moose collisions, and pass remote tourist outliers with names like "The Moose Crossing Gift Shop."

Finally you go over the last low, forested hill, drive past the Indian Hill Shopping Center, and descend toward Greenville and the pretty island-studded south end of Moosehead Lake. Thoreau's description of his first view of the lake holds true, even today:

It is, he wrote, "a suitably wild-looking sheet of water, sprinkled with small low islands . . . covered with shaggy spruce and other wild wood."

Right in the center of town is Thoreau Park, the spot from which Henry, Ed Hoar, and their Indian guide, Joe Polis, pushed off on the early morning of July 24, 1857, for their epic trip into the wild.

The park is a nondescript slice of green wedged in between the road, a gift shop, and the lake. There's a large hand-painted blue sign nearby with some information and some disinformation about the 1857 trip. The sign describes the 1857 journey as "A trip to Katahdin," though it wasn't, and says that Thoreau climbed Mount Kineo via "the knife edge," even though there is no trail or feature by that name on that mountain. (There is a Knife Edge, of course, on Katahdin.) Nearby is another, newer sign with information about the Northern Forest Canoe Trail, a canoe route across the waterways of four states, tracing the ancient routes followed by Native Americans from upstate New York into north-ern Maine. Not coincidentally, it follows part of the route over which the Penobscot leader Joe Polis paddled with Thoreau and Hoar in 1857. That route is today known as the Thoreau-Wabanaki Trail.

On his first trip up Moosehead Lake, in 1853, Thoreau, his cousin George Thatcher, and Joe Aitteon—his Indian guide on that earlier trip—also left from this spot. They rode a steamboat some forty miles up the lake past Mount Kineo, to Northeast Carry, where a short por-tage connects to the West Branch of the Penobscot River. A later steam-boat, the *Katahdin*, quite similar to the steamer Thoreau would have taken, now docks by Thoreau Park and offers regular tours. It is the last steamboat operating on the lake. One tour per year goes as far as Northeast Carry.

Thoreau was a sightseer in 1853, commenting on the wild shores of Moosehead Lake—which are considerably less wild today. Viewing Mount Kineo's steep cliffs, he declared that it would likely be discovered someday that "some Indian maiden" had jumped off the cliff for love, "for true love never could have found a path more to its mind."

In 1857, however, he had paddled all the way up the thirty-mile-long lake, and had no Romantic associations to suggest. In fact, he scorned the Indian legend associated with Kineo—that it was the half-submerged head of a colossal moose (hence the name Moosehead Lake). His account of his Native American guide Joe Polis telling the legend shows Thoreau at his sneering worst. He does not seem to have even wondered whether Polis might have been gently teasing him:

"An Indian tells such a story as if he thought it deserved to have a good deal said about it, only he has not got it to say," he declares, "and so he makes up for the deficiency by a drawling tone, long-windedness, and a dumb wonder which he hopes will be contagious."

The travelers paddled on past the mountain and made camp on its northern shore. Thoreau and Hoar then went back to climb the mountain "along the edge of the precipice." The spectacular trail is still maintained. Today it is called the "Indian Trail."

Thoreau emphasized the wildness of the view and the seemingly limitless forest surrounding him as he and Hoar climbed. "The clouds breaking away a little, we had a glorious wild view, as we ascended, of the broad lake with its fluctuating surface and numerous forest-clad islands," he wrote. "It was a perfect lake of the woods."

He didn't mention, on either of his trips, the presence of the Kineo House, a resort hotel at the base of the mountain. The hotel was built in 1848, before either of Thoreau's trips to Moosehead Lake, and was host to the poet, writer, and editor James Russell Lowell, among other travelers. Lowell enjoyed his five-day stay there and wrote about it in a piece he titled "A Moosehead Journal."

That first hotel burned in 1868 and a second, larger hotel was built, which also burned. The third, largest of the three, was built in 1884 and demolished in 1938, after it had ceased to prosper. A few scattered outbuildings and a golf course remain. Colleen Ashe, a pleasant older woman in 19th-century costume who served as docent at the Greenville Historical Society's Eveleth House museum, remembered not long ago that when she was graduated from Greenville High School, her senior class banquet was held at the last incarnation of the Kineo House. The young Greenville High graduates, all dressed up, had a formal dinner in the old hotel. They went by motorboat across the mile-wide section of the lake that separates Rockville from the Kineo peninsula. The thought of that windy journey pleases me, the young girls going across the choppy lake in formal dresses and corsages, the boys in jackets and ties.

Some seventy or so years later, four of us—two friends, my wife Elizabeth, and I—made the same crossing by motorboat on our way to climb the mountain. It is a dramatically scenic trip with the stony cliffs of the mountain looming above the heaving, windswept lake. One of the few remnants of the grand vacation era that remains on the Kineo peninsula is the 9-hole golf course, ingeniously laid out at the base of the mountain in the 1880s by landscape architect Frederick Law Olmsted. It is still in use today. The clubhouse is a good place to obtain a restorative beer after climbing the mountain.

Though Thoreau studiously ignored the resort hotel, he was fascinated by Kineo's Native American associations, and noted the fact that the mountain, which rises so abruptly from the lake, is a huge plug of hornstone (rhyolite), a flintlike stone that the Penobscots used as arrow and spear points. Artifacts made from Mount Kineo rhyolite have been found all over New England, presumably the result of early Native American trading networks.

Thoreau, experimenting, used a thin, bladelike piece of the stone to cut down an alder, accidentally slashing his fingers in the process. He carefully noted several of the plants he found on his climb up the mountain. Among them were three-toothed cinquefoil, harebells, bearberry, bunchberry, and Canadian blueberry. Since I climbed the mountain at about the same time of year as Thoreau—late July—I was delighted to find several of the same plants, including harebells still drooping their pale, intense blue blossoms beside the trail. It gave me a nice feeling of connection with Henry. But I didn't bother cutting my fingers on the buffy-gray shards of stone along the trail, as he had.

The views from the trail (which it must be confessed include the golf course and regularly passing motorboats) are still strikingly beautiful, an unforgettable mingling of windswept blue waters, dark-forested islands, and great expanses of woodsy northern Maine.

However, the woods are not as wild as they look. These days, there is a paved road along the lake's western edge between Greenville and Rockville, a nice state park at Lily Bay on the east side, and quite a few camps and houses next to the water. "The shore is an unbroken wilderness," Thoreau wrote in 1853. Despite conserved areas, this is no longer so. Pleasantly rustic is more the order of the day.

From Northeast Carry, in both 1853 and 1857, Thoreau and his companions portaged to the West Branch of the Penobscot River—just a mile or so distant—and began paddling downriver to Chesuncook Lake.

Thoreau was interested in Native Americans, and part of the reason for his coming to northern Maine was to see how they lived and hunted. He was a bit disappointed that the guide on his 1853 trip, Joe Aitteon, didn't live up to his Romantic assumptions about Indians. Aitteon had taken on many Yankee ways, whistling popular tunes to himself and exclaiming "Yes-siree!" and "By George!"

That wasn't the only preconception that the trip would shatter for Thoreau. When the moose-hunting that he had come to witness turned from theory to actual bloody fact, he was completely horrified.

They had paddled down the West Branch as far as Pine Stream. Turning up the stream, they saw fresh moose sign, and then two moose: a cow and its calf. George Thatcher, Thoreau's cousin, rose in the canoe and shot at them. Both ran off, but Aitteon found spatters of blood, and followed them. He located the cow moose collapsed in the stream, dead.

"Joe now proceeded to skin the moose with his pocket knife while I looked on," Thoreau wrote. "And a tragical business it was."

Seeing the moose stripped of its "seemly robe" and milk streaming along with blood from the moose's slashed udder shocked Thoreau deeply. The three ate fried moose meat for supper, and then Thatcher and Aitteon went off for more hunting. But Thoreau stayed in camp to botanize and write down his thoughts. The whole savage episode had left him shaken.

"I had had enough of moose hunting," he wrote. "The afternoon's tragedy, and my share in it, as it affected the innocence, destroyed the pleasure of my adventure."

Thoreau's anger and revulsion increased as he wrote. He began to feel that bears, moose, even nature itself were looking at him in reproof for what he began to call "the murder of the moose."

The whole business was, he wrote, "too much like going out by night to some woodside pasture and shooting your neighbor's horses. . . . These are God's own horses, poor timid creatures," he declared, adding angrily: "What a coarse and imperfect use Indians and hunters make of nature! No wonder that their race is so soon exterminated."

His final view of the skinned moose carcass concludes the unpleasant episode. As the three men paddle back down Pine Stream and turn down the West Branch toward Chesuncook Lake, he reports: "We could see the red carcass of the moose lying in Pine Stream when nearly half a mile off." A nightmare vision.

There are almost certainly more moose in New England today than there were in the 1850s. Thoreau and his party actually had to hunt to find a moose. Today, thanks to widespread reforestation and hunting by permit only, moose are everywhere. On the roads of northern Maine, New Hampshire, and Vermont, they are a traffic hazard: there's nothing that will make you respect nature more than a half-ton of moose meat hurtling at you through your shattering windshield.

Moose hunting continues, by permit, in northern New England. When Vermont was first considering a moose hunt, about twenty years ago, the then-speaker of the Vermont House, a Bennington Democrat named Ralph Wright, objected in language that (perhaps unconsciously) echoed Thoreau. Hunting moose, he declared, was not exactly sport. It was more like "shooting a parked car." But the hunt was enacted anyway.

Moose are currently a tangible presence—and a heavily promoted tourist attraction—throughout Maine. They are the official state animal, adopted by the Maine legislature in 1979. But more than that, they fill the role of unofficial mascot or totem, staring goofily from a million coffee mugs, T-shirts, baseball caps, and keychains. There are carved wooden moose, cast plastic and metal moose, stuffed moose dolls wearing lumberjack outfits, and various other moose effigies filling gift shops from Bethel to Lubec. They have become part of Maine's pop culture.

Moose are undeniably thrilling to see. They are prodigiously BIG and ungainly. Their legs are so long and spindly and their heads so enormous, they look vaguely as though they had been assembled from a kit. They project an air of absent-minded docility—quite often they just ignore you, or stare back and watch you watch them. Yet the few encounters I've had with adult bull moose did not make me want to get closer. For all their comic awkwardness, they are huge animals that emit an aura of strength and power.

My closest moose encounter took place on a camping trip in Baxter State Park, where moose presumably know they can't be shot. Some friends and I were hiking back from a night at Wassataquoik Lake to Russell Pond. First we heard a crashing off on the far side of a small pond we were passing, and then very shortly afterward we came upon the source of the noise—a huge bull moose, plodding over the low height of land between two swamps, his long head and immense spread of horns raised high—higher, in fact, than any of us was tall.

There were some dense woods just off the trail on our right. "If he comes at us, drop your packs and run into those woods," I said softly, hoping that the moose wouldn't be able to follow us there.

"Right," said Linda, dropping her pack. "Let's do it now!"

But the moose paid no attention to us whatsoever. Snuffling and snorting gently, he shambled off into the next bog without so much as a glance in our direction. And we resumed our way to Russell Pond.

— — —

Thoreau's outrage over the moose hunt (which he had initially wanted to witness) built into a major Transcendentalist rant as he thought about it and wrote and wrote.

"Every creature is better alive than dead, men and moose and pine trees," he declared. "And he who understands it aright will rather preserve its life than destroy it."

He was especially concerned about pine trees because even in 1853 he saw evidence of the woods being selectively logged, the best and tallest pines being cut down and sawed into lumber. He declared that the "best friend" of the pine tree was not the lumberman who cut it down nor the tanner who skinned off its bark, nor the carpenter nor turpentine-maker.

"No! no! it is the poet; he it is who makes the truest use of the pine— who does not fondle it with an axe, nor tickle it with a saw, nor stroke it with a plane. . . ."

He makes it clear who "the poet" is: that would be himself. "It is the living spirit of the tree, not its spirit of turpentine, with which I sympathize, and which heals my cuts," he writes. "It is as immortal as I am and perchance will go to as high a heaven, there to tower above me still."

That passage, inoffensive as it seems to us today, was red-penciled by James Russell Lowell, the editor of the *Atlantic*, when he published Thoreau's essay "Chesuncook" in the magazine.

As he read Thoreau's manuscript, Lowell apparently decided that the Transcendentalist notion of a pine tree having an immortal soul eligible for heaven would be too shocking for the proper readers of the *Atlantic*, and deleted the sentence. But Thoreau wanted it left in. When he saw the proofs, he firmly marked the deletion "stet" ("let it stand"). But Lowell did not restore it, and published the essay with the pine tree noble but not divine, and certainly not bound for his proper Bostonian heaven.

Thoreau was outraged. He sent Lowell a seething letter, and never wrote for the *Atlantic* again while Lowell was editor.

Thoreau's 1853 party made their way down the West Branch of the Penobscot to Chesuncook Lake. There at the northwest end of the lake, he stayed at Ansel Smith's logging camp—a spacious, low, log building which no longer exists. The legend at the Lake House is that Thoreau slept under his boat down by the landing. But Thoreau himself disputes that, noting in his essay that he slept in Smith's log building and was kept awake at night by the sound of people creaking their way across the rough plank floor.

It was raining steadily in June of 1853, and so the party returned up the West Branch to Northeast Carry, where they camped overnight with a group of Indians—and then rode the steamer back down the lake the next day, past Mount Kineo.

One pleasantly rustic establishment just north of Mount Kineo today is The Birches, a woodsy lodge on Moosehead Lake's west shore, near Rockwood. Cabins and yurts, canoes and fishing boats can be rented there, and large captive trout swim round and round in an open tank in the foyer. Elizabeth and I had a pleasantly rustic dinner in the log-cabin-style, candlelit dining room one July night, as the glossy lake lapped peacefully on the dock outside.

On the porch sat a half dozen young men and women, nursing beers and quietly bantering after a day of fishing. A canoe slipped silently by on the opalescent waters, with Kineo's looming bulk rising across the lake to the south. The northeastern arm of Moosehead Lake led off into the twilit distance toward Northeast Carry.

The Birches' pleasant, small-scale, nature-oriented approach to tourism may soon be an anachronism. Plum Creek, a national land and timber corporation, has announced plans to unleash a huge, multifaceted development that would establish 975 house lots, two major resorts, three recreational vehicle parks, a golf course, marina, and rental cabins along the shores of Moosehead and surrounding lakes.

The plans call for rezoning more than 400,000 acres of land in and around Greenville and Rockwood. It is the largest development proposal in Maine history, and has been engendered by changing patterns of land ownership in the Maine woods—plus the fact that a lot of the great forest is pretty much logged out. New ways of making a profit from the land are being sought.

The general assumption in Greenville is that the Plum Creek development will almost certainly be approved in some form—perhaps slightly smaller than proposed. In any case, it will change the low-key, down-home style of tourism that Moosehead Lake now enjoys.

It is a controversial topic in the region. That is because it offers economic activity, perhaps even a measure of prosperity—something the region has had precious little of in recent years—along with the inevitable social and environmental upheaval. The Greenville town clerk politely refers inquiries to the local company spokesman, and some Greenville residents lower their voices and look around carefully before expressing an opinion. Everyone knows that for better or worse, change, probably major change, is coming to Moosehead Lake.

At the other end of the environmental/political spectrum is the long-standing proposal to protect this huge region with an equally huge Maine Woods National Park. The specter of change, which dominates the entire region, is also driving the national park idea.

"It's not that different now from when Thoreau was there," says Michael Kellett, executive director of Restore: The North Woods, the organization backing the national park proposal. "But it's not going to stay that way."

Something about the Maine woods must make people think big. Restore: The North Woods has proposed a national park the size of Connecticut that would encompass most of this vast upland area. It's a proposal that raises at least as many hackles as the Plum Creek development. Not the same hackles, however.

At 3.2 million acres the park would be bigger than Yellowstone and Yosemite combined. If created it would stretch from Maine's western border with Canada all the way south and west to Baxter State Park, including the wild lands around Moosehead and Chesuncook lakes, Chamberlain Lake, the headwaters of the St. John River, and the Allagash Waterway. Kellett is careful to point out that all of Baxter State Park, Katahdin included, would remain under Maine's jurisdiction if the national park is created.

Nearly everyone agrees that's a pretty big if. The park seems to have almost zero traction in the real world at this point. There is no bill in Congress. No U.S. senator or representative has endorsed the proposal, and Maine's current governor, John Baldacci, firmly opposes it. Kellett is fond of saying that for the cost of one B-1 bomber, the land could be bought and the park established. But that's still about a billion dollars, and Washington continues to show more interest in military hardware than in preserving the Maine woods.

Kellett admits the forest he would protect has been heavily logged.

"It looks like a national park with clear-cuts," he says, without cracking a smile.

The regenerative powers of the Northern Forest will help the land recover, if only it can be protected, he says, but adds: "If there's no acquisition, the land is going to get trashed."

Actually, there's already a fair amount of land protection happening in the Maine woods. Between federal and state land purchases, conservation easements, and privately conserved lands, almost one-third of the area encompassed by the national park proposal already has some degree of protection from development or unrestricted logging. But key sections—huge key sections—of the area remain open to major developments such as the Plum Creek proposal. The wild character of the area could change drastically within the next twenty years.

"It's a patchwork now," says Kellett. "Is it going to be one big protected area, or will it remain a patchwork?"

Well, yes. That is precisely the question that hovers over this huge area: what is the future of the Maine woods?

— — —

A century ago, the same question hovered over Katahdin. Thoreau had been dead a half-century and the forests on and around Katahdin were devastated by logging and forest fires. It took another visionary bachelor—a man very different from Thoreau—to save the mountain. That was Percival P. Baxter, governor, conservationist, millionaire, and an environmental activist: quintessentially the right man at the right time.

Baxter, heir to a canning company fortune and well connected, had gone into politics. He had fallen in love with the Maine wilds, and especially with Katahdin. He was first elected to the Maine legislature in 1904, where he began his political career. What followed was one of the great conservation sagas in American history.

From the beginning, he was interested in land conservation. By 1919, he had entered a bill in the Maine legislature to buy Katahdin and make it the centerpiece of a state park. But the legislature, bound to timbering interests and chronically myopic, repeatedly refused. Though Baxter became governor in 1920, he couldn't force the bill through.

"Having in mind that the people of Maine once owned these great areas of timberland," he wrote, "is it not fitting that, upon payment of a fair price . . . the grandest and most beautiful portion of all this great area which the people of the state once possessed, should again become their property?"

The Maine legislature responded with a firm no, several times, to various proposals.

However, Percival Baxter was a man of near-legendary stubbornness. In 1930, after leaving the governor's office, he began personally buying up the land he wanted to protect. Over the course of the next forty years, he acquired parcel after parcel on and around his beloved mountain. Thus, Baxter himself bought Katahdin and its surrounding lands, and gave it as a state park to the people of Maine. He was eighty-seven years old when he concluded his efforts. His twenty-eight purchases eventually totaled more than 200,000 acres, which Baxter conserved in strictly worded deeds of trust. Katahdin and the land around it, he said, must remain forever wild: no paved roads, no food concessions, no big lodges or sprawling parking lots, only primitive trails and shelters. And so it remains today. Baxter described his life's work with feeling in 1941:

"Katahdin stands above the surrounding plain unique in grandeur and glory. The works of man are short-lived. Monuments decay, buildings crumble, and wealth vanishes, but Katahdin will forever remain the mountain of the people of Maine. Throughout the ages it will stand as an inspiration to the men and women of this state."

Today, the highest peak on the mountain is named Baxter Peak, and the great park which surrounds the mountain also bears his name. It is a fitting tribute to the man who saved New England's greatest mountain.

Noble as Baxter's actions were, the story of his devotion to the mountain illustrates an unpleasant factor in the history of the northern woods:

the state of Maine, until recently, had a massively undistinguished record in protecting its most important wild lands. For a long time, Maine had one of the lowest percentages of conserved land in the United States. More recently, through the Land for Maine's Future program, that trend has been reversed. But until the establishment of that program in 1987, Maine's record in protecting its natural treasures was not good.

The reason is obvious: historically, the state's great northern wilderness was mostly owned by large timber and paper companies, which had enormous political clout. They logged the woods, but left large areas open for hunters, fishermen, canoers, and hikers. Thus, Maine's wilderness was made available for the use of the people by the paternalistic authority of the paper companies. It was a quiet tradeoff: we take the timber we need and you can sport on the unharvested lands.

This worked, at least for Maine, until the late 20th century, when global economics of the timber industry and the near-exhaustion of the resource itself induced the paper/timber companies to sell off their lands in the Northern Forest. In the 1980s and 1990s, huge tracts of land went on the market. Since that time, according to Restore's Michael Kellett, more than seven million acres of land have been sold at least once. Those sales destabilized Maine's forest lands and raised the specter of massive development throughout the North Country. The huge Plum Creek development proposed around Moosehead Lake is the region's first— but probably not its last—such proposal. Likewise, the Maine Woods National Park idea was generated, at least in part, by that same tectonic shift in land ownership.

There are strong opponents to the proposed national park, even to the idea of more conserved land. (Even Percival Baxter might have opposed a national park—he fiercely fought against establishing such a park around Katahdin because he didn't trust the federal government to preserve the mountain in its pristine state. However, Baxter would certainly have favored more conserved lands.) Traditional timbermen, snowmobilers, ATV riders, and some hunters and fishermen, especially, see the proposed park as a threat. The economy of the North Woods has been based on two resource-based activities—logging and recreation. Both industries have become more nervous as it increasingly appears the resource is running out.

In the meantime, conservation efforts have continued. Maine's citizens have demonstrated on several occasions that they want conserved lands and are willing to tax themselves to pay for them. In 1987, they voted a bond issue of $35 million to help fund the Land for Maine's Future program. In 1999, they voted it an additional $50 million. And, in 2005, they voted for $12 million more. That money was used with other private and foundation money to protect several hundred thousand acres of land in the North Woods and elsewhere.

There has been opposition. A wealthy conservationist, Roxanne Quimby, has been personally attacked and ridiculed for following a course very similar to Percival Baxter's. Ms. Quimby, who made a fortune manufacturing and selling her "Burt's Bees" lip balms and skin creams, has bought up, as of this writing, some 75,000 acres of northern Maine forest land near Baxter State Park, much of which she plans to protect as wilderness. For her efforts she has been vilified and become a lightning rod for opposition to the park idea.

There is little doubt that Henry David Thoreau would approve of more conservation, probably the national park also, at least in some form. Near the end of his "Chesuncook" essay, he launched into a passionate defense of wild lands. He concluded with a plea—one of the first in America—for national parks to preserve wild places like northern Maine.

"Not only for strength, but for beauty," he declares, "the poet must, from time to time, travel the logger's path and the Indian's trail, to drink at some new and more bracing fountain of the Muses, far in the recesses of the wilderness."

The kings of England, he noted, sometimes destroyed villages to protect their lands and game. "Why should not we, who have renounced the king's authority, have our national preserves, where no village need be destroyed, in which the bear and the panther, and some even of the hunter race, may still exist, and not be 'civilized off the face of the earth'. . . not for idle sport or food, but for inspiration and our own true recreation?

"Or shall we, like villains, grub them all up, poaching upon our own national domains?"

It's interesting that Thoreau's vision included villages and hunters as well as wild lands: a mix, in other words. Perhaps . . . a patchwork?

— — —

Thoreau described his descent of the West Branch of the Penobscot toward Chesuncook Lake in 1853 as follows:

"You paddle along in a narrow canal through an endless forest," he wrote. "The vision I have in my mind's eye, still, is of the small dark and sharp tops of tall fir and spruce trees, and pagoda-like arbor-vitaes, crowded together on each side, with various hard woods intermixed."

It is still an apt description, but the river is tamer today than it was in the 1850s. There are numerous campsites along the West Branch today and, in the summer, they are often filled. Below Pine Stream (where Thatcher shot the moose) there used to be two heavy stretches of whitewater known as Pine Stream Falls. Thoreau portaged around them on both his 1853 and 1857 trips while his Indian guides ran the canoe through the rapids. Chesuncook Dam, built in 1903–04, raised the level of Chesuncook Lake enough to cover Pine Stream Falls, and the 1916 Ripogenus Dam raised it even more. Today above Chesuncook Lake the West Branch is a pleasant stretch of smooth water with established campsites alongside. It is an easy paddle, and so attracts many paddlers and campers.

The dams on the West Branch and others were built by lumbermen so they could float timber out of the then-roadless Maine woods. River drives of the 19th and early 20th century were legendary tests of skill and manhood, and the rough stretches—the rapids—often drowned loggers. Joe Aitteon, Thoreau's 1853 guide—the good-natured Indian who whistled "Oh Susannah"—was a logger by trade and was tragically drowned in 1870 at Grand Falls, on the West Branch.

The Indian name "Chesuncook" means "a place where many streams flow together," and, before the first dam was built in 1840, that accurately described the northern end of what was then an open valley—a wide, grassy meadow with the river flowing southward through it.

The series of dams that was built downriver gradually enlarged the lake, and Ripogenus Dam raised the water level substantially, covering all the previous dams and merging the southern end of Chesuncook Lake with Caribou and Ripogenus lakes. Chesuncook is now more than twenty miles long and is the third largest lake in Maine.

Dams were built throughout northern Maine, and logging runs down the rivers continued until 1976 when environmental concerns and changing timber practices ended them. The paper companies subsequently built some 20,000 miles of logging roads.

On his first excursions, Thoreau apparently had some favorable feelings toward Maine's lumbermen. He referred to them as "redbirds" on account of the red flannel shirts they wore, and speculated that they were adventurous and free of society's restraints because they lived in the woods. But by 1857 his enthusiasm had waned. He was well acquainted with the loggers' system of dams and, as he, Polis, and Hoar paddled Chamberlain Lake, he noted that the dams had drowned the shoreline trees, leaving that lake—and others like it—with a belt of standing deadwood that destroyed the natural shore.

"They have thus dammed all the larger lakes, raising their broad surfaces many feet," he wrote, "turning the forces of nature against herself, that they might float their spoils out of the country. . . . Think how much land they have flowed without asking Nature's leave," he grumbled. In "The Allagash and the East Branch," his account of his 1857 trip that concludes *The Maine Woods*, he described the loggers themselves as "10,000 vermin, gnawing at the base of her noblest trees."

At the north end of Chesuncook Lake, where the West Branch of the Penobscot River empties in, lies just the sort of tiny village Thoreau might have had in mind when he noted that in his ideal park "no village need be destroyed." After the Civil War, Ansel Smith's logging camp developed into the village of Chesuncook.

In 1853 Thoreau stopped at Chesuncook and stayed at Smith's camp, which was primitive enough at that time to be interesting to him. The bay at which Thoreau docked seemed archaic and mythical to him: "Such a one, methought, as the Argo might have launched in." He thought the camp itself, a rambling log building eighty feet long, had "a very rich and picturesque look" because it was built with logs and had no pretensions or ornamentation. He described its accommodations wryly as being "a slight departure from the hollow tree."

Thoreau made some persnickety remarks about the crudeness of the loggers' conversation, and declared that for his dessert after dinner, "I helped myself to a large slice of the Chesuncook woods, and took a hearty draught of its waters with all my senses." He accurately predicted that a settlement would likely grow at Chesuncook. "Such were the first rude beginnings of a town," he noted.

In 1864, two years after Thoreau's death, seven years after his last visit there, the Great Northern Paper Company built a large, plain, three-story house at Chesuncook to house its loggers. The building later became the Chesuncook Lake House, which now operates as an inn, perhaps the quietest, most relaxing inn in the Northeast. Elizabeth and I spent a night there, justifying the pleasant escape as "research."

Over the years, the small village grew. It prospered with the lumbering trade and though it never had more than a couple dozen residents, it eventually acquired a church and a school. Ansel Smith's grave is in the little cemetery nearby; the church was restored and rededicated in 1975. Its wood-paneled interior radiates a warm, simple spirituality—the sort of Christian piety that Thoreau would have none of—and a scrapbook in the vestibule notes that Chesuncook Village "all but died out" after World War II. The little church and the Chesuncook Lake House are now on the National Register of Historic Places.

A one-lane road leads from the landing to the former village through stands of scrubby forest with occasional views of the lake. A half-century ago, it led through open fields, but time and the inexorable march of the forest are closing them. At "The Store," which is announced by a prominent sign, Jack Murphy sells fudge, root beer, and toilet paper to campers and canoers. The store seems to be entirely contained on the enclosed sun porch of Murphy's small house. The root beer comes fresh-bottled right out of his porch refrigerator, and the fudge is very sweet. "Keep the faith!" he says cheerily as we depart, sugared up.

Beyond Murphy's little store, a few camps line the rudimentary road, which simplifies itself into a trail that leads a mile through rough third- or fourth-growth woods to a campsite over on the West Branch of the Penobscot. The campsite is called "boom house," for the logging boom and gatehouse once located there, a couple of hundred yards from the West Branch's entry into the enlarged Chesuncook Lake. The actual house has been moved a few miles down the west shore of the lake, where it now does duty as a private camp. Along the lake's rocky shores, you can still find hefty chunks of logging hardware—massive bolts sunk in the rock attached to thick iron rings a foot or more in diameter. They are remnants of the system of booms and other implements used to corral, measure, and transport millions of logs south, down the lake and into the lower West Branch, bound for Bangor.

You can also see the lake's logging heritage in the long, narrow dining room of the Chesuncook Lake House, with its pressed-tin walls and ceiling, where a gang of hungry loggers regularly sat down to supper after their long days of work in the woods. The Lake House is now run by David and Luisa Suprenant, a pleasant young couple of easygoing manner and seemingly boundless energy. The Suprenants and their five children make up seventy percent of Chesuncook's current year-round population of ten. The previous owners, Maggie and Bert McBurnie, owned and ran the Chesuncook Lake House for roughly a half century before the Suprenants bought it in 1998.

Luisa and David were living in Massachusetts when David discovered Chesuncook Village in 1992. The quiet northern end of Chesuncook Lake kept calling to him and he kept coming back. In 1994, he telephoned Luisa and said she had to come up and see the place. When she did that, she didn't want to leave.

"I said, 'Can't we just call my mother and have her drive the kids up here?' " she recalls.

Five years later, Bert McBurnie had died, and Maggie sold Chesuncook Lake House to the Suprenants. They haven't looked back.

On clear days, the view from the porch of the Lake House is big and wild, a hypnotically beautiful swath of lake and forest. Some thirty miles to the south rises the rugged blue bulk of Katahdin and the blue folds of lesser peaks surrounding it. There's no radio, no TV, no Internet, no e-mail. The rooms have no telephone, and a modest amount of electricity is supplied by the inn's own generator. At Chesuncook, you are definitely off the grid.

"There's nothing to do here," Luisa says happily. "So people sit on the porch."

It is an excuse—sometimes unplanned—for letting the rest of the world go by. A loon was calling from somewhere out on the lake as Luisa took an unaccustomed break and sat with us and talked.

There's actually quite a lot to do at Chesuncook, but the place is definitely disconnected from the rest of plugged-in American life. Sitting on the porch without the distractions most of the world accepts as modern life seems like a gift. A steady flow of guests keeps Luisa and David busy, year-round.

Nobody blunders onto Chesuncook Village. You have to want to be there to find the place. Fishing, camping, family reunions with time for actual conversation, hiking, solitude—and, in the winter, snowmobiling, snowshoeing, and cross-country skiing are the attractions.

In fact, after a week or more of rain, simple dryness can also be an attraction—warmth, shelter, and showers. "Canoers come here after a couple of days on the river and beg me to put them anywhere," Luisa says. "Anywhere—in the attic, under a rock—just get me out of this rain!"

After almost ten years of running the place, it has become home for the Suprenants, and their livelihood.

"I can't imagine living anyplace else. I was never comfortable down there," Luisa says, meaning Massachusetts. "This was home right away."

The Suprenants seem as enterprising and independent as it is possible to be in the United States today. They have enlarged the house to make room for their substantial family, and Luisa homeschools their children. When their two older girls reached high school age, they were given the choice of continuing homeschooling or boarding out and attending public high school fifty miles south in Dover-Foxcroft. The two girls chose that option, primarily to have more of a social life than Chesuncook Village offers.

Raising her children is not a secondary occupation for Luisa Suprenant. It's part of the reason she has so completely embraced Chesuncook. "I want to teach my children to be self-reliant," she says. "Not to rely on anyone but themselves. Nowadays, things are so programmed for most kids."

She also wants her children to enjoy being children, not to have every minute scheduled and be under constant pressure. That was one of the things that she disliked about life down-country. Life is simpler in Chesuncook, play is simpler. When the family got a new dryer, the big cardboard box it came packaged in was "the greatest thing," she recalls. Despite the lack of steady playmates, in some ways Chesuncook Village has to be a kid's dream come true—woods, a lake, dogs, a horse, and a motorized doodlebug to putter around in.

It's less of an idyll for the adults who run the place. There is a lot of work involved. David seems to be the outside guy—he takes care of maintenance and chores, runs the motorboat shuttle down-lake, and drives the big Army surplus truck to town for supplies over unmarked logging roads. Luisa, in addition to homeschooling the children, tends the garden, makes the meals, and runs the business side of the Lake House.

They are an impressive couple, David affable, laid-back, quietly competent; Luisa friendly, but focused and no-nonsense. Without perhaps knowing it, they are living their lives as Thoreau chose to live his—self-reliantly, according to their values. In a word, deliberately.

The forest, lake, and mountains surround them with mile upon mile of wildness—developed, undeveloped, logged, unlogged, and recovering. Growing. Changing. Transforming itself, year by year. The Suprenants came here not to search that wildness to its core, as Thoreau did, but simply because they loved it. Another of Thoreau's motives—a conscious retreat to escape from a conventionally regimented existence—seems closer to what keeps them here.

The larger world comes to them in small doses, by boat or the occasional seaplane. They seem to get just about as much of it as they want or need. They do not seem lonely. They are not Thoreau groupies or Thoreau scholars.

But he would, I am sure, recognize and admire them.

I was comparatively satisfied. There I had got the Cape under me, as much as if I were riding it bare-backed. It was not as on the map, or seen from the stage-coach; but there I found it all out-of-doors, huge and real, Cape Cod! as it cannot be represented on a map, color it as you will; the thing itself, than which there is nothing more like it, no truer picture or account; which you cannot go farther and see. I cannot remember what I thought before that it was.

—Cape Cod

7

Walking Cape Cod

The ironies of history echo across Cape Cod.

When Henry David Thoreau, America's first great environmentalist, went to the Cape in 1849, it was a near-complete environmental disaster: almost treeless, its eroded and overgrazed topsoil mostly gone, its sands blowing into the ocean.

And Thoreau loved it.

Further, it was a 19th-century killing ground. The Atlantic relentlessly pounded hundreds, even thousands of ships into rubble on the Cape's outer bars. The beach was desolate and grim.

And Thoreau loved that, too.

"It is a wild, rank place, and there is no flattery in it," he wrote in his book *Cape Cod*. "The carcasses of men and beasts together lie stately up upon its shelf, rotting and bleaching in the sun and waves, and each tide turns them in their beds, and tucks fresh sand under them. There is naked Nature—inhumanly sincere, wasting no thought on man, nibbling at the cliffy shore where gulls wheel amid the spray."

Visitors to the Cape's Outer Beach today will not find corpses on the beach—at least not human ones. Yet they will find something profoundly beautiful, deeply awe-inspiring. For the Outer Beach is one of the most dramatic and extended seascapes in America—a broad strip of sand backed by a steep glacial bluff that extends some twenty-eight miles facing the wild Atlantic in an unbroken, curving swath from Nauset Marsh in Eastham to Race Point and the Province Lands.

Of course, it is no longer the remote outpost that Thoreau walked. "A man may stand there and put all America behind him," he wrote, happily summing up his Cape Cod experiences. Today that hardly seems true. At least not at first glance.

Any local Cape Cod newspaper, like newspapers all over the country, contains stories detailing the latest drug threat or recovery program, the latest mega-development working its way through the regulatory process, the latest pollution threat or quiver in real estate prices. (At this writing, the median price of a house in Wellfleet is more than $600,000.)

Whatever it was then, today the Cape is emphatically part of America, part of the 21st-century economic engine of recreation and tourism.

Not all of the changes brought by the intervening 150 years have been damaging. Thanks to the National Seashore, much of outer Cape Cod is unspoiled and open. But even with that protection, the Cape today is very different from the place that Thoreau visited in 1849, 1850, and 1855. The Cape then had been stripped of most of its native forest and reduced to a huge, nearly barren sandspit; it was literally coming apart at the seams, blowing randomly into the sea.

"The barren aspect of the land would hardly be believed, if described," Thoreau wrote in *Cape Cod*.

Near the Nauset Lights (there were three in the mid-1800s), he described the landscape through which he and his friend the poet Ellery Channing were walking: "We found ourselves at once on an apparently boundless plain, without a tree or a fence, or even, with one or two exceptions, a house in sight."

The few remaining trees were dwarfed. Thoreau describes apple trees no higher than a man and some that looked like potted plants, "not much larger than currant-bushes."

By the time they had walked along the Outer Beach as far as North Truro, the barrenness was almost universal. There were hardly any trees at all and the bare contours of the land left by the glacier and amended by the winds were exposed. Looking from Highland Light across the Cape's narrow "wrist," Thoreau could see every individual hillock and valley, carpeted only with tiny shrubs and heath plants. He could clearly see Cape Cod Bay beyond, the view completely unobstructed.

The primary road, he noted, was merely a pair of tracks through the sand. "Poverty grass" (*Hudsonia tomentosa*) and seaside goldenrod were everywhere, and Thoreau, comically perverse, proposed that poverty grass be made the official crest of Barnstable County, perhaps especially because the Cape Codders disliked it.

"This peculiar open country, with here and there a patch of shrubbery, extends as much as seven miles, or from Pamet River on the south to High Head on the north, and from Ocean to Bay," he wrote. "It is as wild and solitary as the Western Prairies used to be."

The cause of that near-universal barrenness was the Cape Codders themselves. Over the years, they had cut down nearly every tree for fuel and allowed their cattle and sheep to overgraze the rest of the land. They had wiped out virtually all the original forest cover. The thin layer of original topsoil was gone. The Outer Cape—Eastham, Wellfleet, Truro, and the Province Lands—had become a textbook case of soil erosion.

Photographs taken in the latter 19th century show the resulting bleakness clearly, a blowing wilderness of open sand. In places the wind piled the loose sand into dunes, which blew hither and yon, adding to the desertlike appearance of the place. (C-shaped parabolic dunes are a feature of today's Province Lands.)

Thoreau took special note of the widespread erosion, entitling one chapter of *Cape Cod* "The Sea and the Desert." He also observed the residents' early attempts at conservation—the systematic planting of pitch pines in Truro and beach grass around Provincetown. Careful botanical observer that he was, he noted that the beach grass would arrest the blowing sand and then grow up through it, anchoring the restless dune in place.

"Thus Cape Cod is anchored to the heavens, as it were, by a myriad little cables of beach-grass, and, if they should fail, would become a total wreck, and erelong go to the bottom," he wrote.

In Truro, Thoreau saw planted rows of pitch pine, another strategy for stabilizing the Cape's blowing sands. He described the planting methods in detail, noting that the horse-drawn planting machine left a spiral furrow that descended into the barren hollows.

"This experiment, so important to the Cape, appeared very successful," he wrote. "And perhaps the time will come when the greater part of this kind of land in Barnstable County will be thus covered with an artificial pine forest."

As every visitor to the Cape today can see, that is exactly what happened. Over most of the Cape, pitch pines are the dominant tree, and when you drive Route 6 out toward Provincetown you go through a mature planted forest of pitch pines. If you turn east off the main road in Wellfleet or Truro, and drive through that forest toward the Great Beach, the pines, interspersed with scrub oak, become smaller and smaller toward the final bluff. Only in the last few hundred yards before the ocean are the pines replaced by low heath plants—bearberry, bog cranberry, poverty grass, seaside goldenrod, beach grass.

And then the broad sweep of the Great Beach and the immense, restless ocean appears, just as Thoreau would have seen it.

I first walked the Outer Beach of Cape Cod more than thirty years ago. I had decided to do so after reading *Cape Cod* for the first time. Thoreau's vivid writing was too compelling not to go.

One day I walked southward from Race Point to our rented cabin in South Wellfleet. The next day, tired, sore, and unable to walk much at all, I looked at the ocean. The day after that, I completed my walk to Nauset Marsh. Since then, on shorter jaunts, I have walked most of that twenty-eight miles again, some sections several times.

What I have found is that despite the crowding, the over-development, the obvious damage to some places, the Outer Beach that Thoreau so obviously loved still retains its rugged beauty and power to enthrall.

The great, tawny rampart of the high bluff still faces the wind and sea, still glows gold in the morning sunlight and rests in deep blue shadows in the evening. Beach grass still trembles in the wind and its tips still draw the perfect circles in the sand that Thoreau admired. The long days of summer, the short days of autumn and winter still fill the vast spaces with an eloquent, glowing light that makes the heart ache with beauty. And, yes, rain and fog still wrap the Cape in gray mystery on many days, wind and storms still drive the sea inexorably against the beach, as it has been relentlessly driven for the last eight thousand or so years.

The Atlantic has been pounding the entire eastern shore of the Cape since it was formed by the receding continental glacier, grinding and gnawing away chunks of the bank and the beach every year. In fact, if you were today to walk the exact path taken by Thoreau and Channing in 1849, you would have to walk in the ocean—more than a hundred yards offshore.

The beach—and the cape behind it—is not truly wild, nor is it completely tame. It is today, as it was in Thoreau's day, a place apart, an open strip of sand and beach heather that stands between the human world of the Cape itself, and the true wilderness that is the Atlantic Ocean.

Cape Cod thrusts farther out into the ocean than any other portion of the Atlantic coast in this hemisphere. The possibility of walking all of that great expanse of curving Outer Beach caught Thoreau's fancy and drew him there. He wanted to get to know the ocean better, he wrote. In 1849, he went for his first walk on the Cape with Ellery Channing.

They had intended to take the regular steamer to Provincetown and hike from there south to Orleans, and then back west to the Massachusetts mainland. However, a severe storm kept their boat in Boston, so Thoreau and Channing went to the Cape by train, traveled by stagecoach from Sandwich to Orleans, and then began walking north.

The same storm that had delayed their boat had fatally wrecked another on the rocks of Cohasset, killing 145 people, mostly Irish immigrants. Thoreau and Channing stopped on their way to the Cape and visited the grim aftermath, which Thoreau describes crisply and graphically in the opening chapter of *Cape Cod:*

"I saw many marble feet and matted heads as the cloths were raised, and one livid, swollen, and mangled body of a drowned girl,—who probably had intended to go out to service in some American family,—to which some rags still adhered, with a string, half-concealed by the flesh, about its swollen neck; the coiled-up wreck of a human hulk, gashed by the rocks or fishes, so that the bone and muscle were exposed, but quite bloodless,—merely red and white,—with wide-open and staring eyes, yet lustreless, dead-lights; or like the cabin windows of a stranded vessel, filled with sand. . . ."

After viewing the shipwreck and its corpses, after a long stagecoach ride, and a night in an Orleans tavern, they began walking northward, across the open Nauset plains. It was raining.

Yet ironically, the blowing storm through which he and Channing walked only made him more exuberant.

Thoreau loved being right next to to the elemental wildness of the North Atlantic. In his day, the sea off Cape Cod was a deadly wrecking ground, and the Outer Beach was a near-deserted graveyard. Storms often drove ships struggling along the coast onto the Cape's outer bars, pounded them to bits and drowned their crews and passengers. Estimates suggest that more than three thousand ships have been sunk or destroyed along the Outer Beach. And so the roar of the untamed ocean and the destruction it causes are a constant theme throughout *Cape Cod.*

"On the whole, we were glad of the storm, which would show us the ocean in its angriest mood," he wrote. "My spirits rose in proportion to the outward dreariness."

Most of all, Thoreau was happy to have escaped the towns and to have left behind "the bar-rooms of Massachusetts." The towns need ventilation, he declared tartly. The gods would not be appeased with cigar smoke.

Much of the "Plains of Nauset" in Eastham over which Thoreau and Channing plodded are today almost completely developed. Instead of an open, desolate plain, there are vacation homes and landscaped back yards.

However, there are places where it is possible to view the open heathland and long views that delighted Thoreau. One such view can be had from the hilltop viewing platform at the Marconi Station historic site in South Wellfleet. And it is possible, by amending their route somewhat, to walk from a point near where Thoreau and Channing "left the road" and proceed from the National Seashore's Salt Pond visitor center (located on busy Route 6) via hiking trails out past pretty Nauset Marsh to Coast Guard Beach. The major difference is that today, you walk not across an open, sandy plain, but through a shady pine forest. After a mile or so, you will cross an arm of the Nauset salt marsh on a wooden bridge, and approach the beach on the small hill occupied by the old Coast Guard station.

This undeniably scenic spot connects with another thread in the Cape's literary history: the sand spit visible off to the southeast is where the writer Henry Beston lived in a tiny Walden-like cabin for a year and wrote *The Outermost House*. Beston's cabin was washed out to sea in the huge winter storm of 1978; the sand barrier beach and the salt marsh remain. The view from the hill by the Coast Guard station is the first of many striking vistas of land and ocean that await today's walker. To the south, Nauset Marsh lies green and fertile behind the protective barrier beach. To the north, the familiar configuration of the steep bluff first appears, facing the broad beach and the restless Atlantic itself.

"There was nothing but that savage ocean between us and Europe," Thoreau wrote, describing his first view of the Atlantic from the top of the glacial bluff in Eastham. He was exhilarated.

Looking out over the wild ocean, whatever preconceptions about Cape Cod Thoreau may have had were blown away by the stormy Atlantic wind. "I cannot remember what I thought before that it was," he wrote.

"I was comparatively satisfied. There I had got the Cape under me, as much as if I were riding it bare-backed. It was not as on the map, or seen from the stage-coach; but there I found it all out-of-doors, huge and real, Cape Cod! as it cannot be represented on a map, color it as you will; the thing itself, than which there is . . . no truer picture or account; which you cannot go farther and see."

He and Channing quickly clambered down the steep face of the bluff to get as close as they could to the stormy ocean. Then they began walking northward, toward Provincetown, delighted with the bad weather and the roaring surf. Observing the stormy sea, Thoreau plunged into the collective unconscious and emerged with an eternal simile, describing the inward-charging waves with an image used since the time of Homer:

"The breakers looked like droves of a thousand wild horses of Neptune, rushing to the shore, with their white manes streaming far behind," he wrote, adding that strands of kelp were tossed up in the spray "like tails of sea-cows sporting in the brine."

The two men made their way along the beach, then along the bluff, then back on the beach, watching the sea break violently over the outer bars, talking occasionally with "wreckers" (beachcombers), marveling at the barren, elementally simple landscape. They were completely absorbed in the experience, entranced and happy. Thoreau's prose turns light and playful, and he tosses in quotations in Greek from Homer, noting:

"I put in a little Greek now and then, partly because it sounds so much like the ocean,—though," he adds patriotically, "I doubt if Homer's *Mediterranean* Sea ever sounded so loud as this."

Today, it is virtually impossible to follow Thoreau's example and split your walk between the beach and the bank-top. The National Seashore, for perfectly good reasons involving safety and erosion, prohibits walking along the bluff for much of the distance above the Great Beach. And because there are numerous inholdings within the National Seashore, walking along on the bluff-top often means trespassing on private property.

Consequently, for most of the twenty-eight miles north and west from Coast Guard Beach, travelers must walk on the beach itself. However, there are places to sample the view from the top of the bluff, and the basic architecture of the Outer Cape, the structure that makes it so dramatically beautiful, is almost inescapable. Wherever you approach the Great Beach in Eastham, Wellfleet, or Truro, you are likely to encounter the stunning swath of brown sand and vast blue ocean that captured Thoreau and Channing 150 years ago and drew them back to the Outer Beach again and again.

— — —

Thoreau had visited the monument (which still stands) in Truro's town cemetery, "Sacred to the Memory of 57 Citizens of Truro who were lost on seven vessels which foundered at sea in the memorable gale of Oct. 3, 1841." Talking to an elderly wrecker, Thoreau observed that the man must like to hear the surf pounding—it presumably meant wreckage and income to him. "No, I do not like to hear the sound of the surf," the old man replied. He had lost a son in the 1841 gale.

"The stranger and the inhabitant view the shore with very different eyes," Thoreau, the stranger, wrote. "The former may have come to see and admire the ocean in a storm; but the latter looks on it as the scene where his nearest relatives were wrecked."

The violence of the ocean, its capacity for death and destruction, underscored its sublimity—a quality any good 19th-century Romantic would treasure.

But Thoreau's happiness as he walked along the Atlantic was more than merely fashionable or philosophical. His sandy steps lightened and his spirit rose, simply because he was close to the profound wild energy of the sea. Despite the reputation of the Outer Beach, despite the desolation he chronicles, *Cape Cod* is not a gloomy book. On the contrary, it is often lighthearted and humorous. (Much of it was written originally as lectures, and they were apparently a hit: his friend

Ralph Waldo Emerson noted that Thoreau's listeners were convulsed with laughter.)

As he approached a "Charity House" near Cahoon Hollow in Wellfleet, his prose reflected his lightheartedness. He was in a jocular mood as he inspected the grim little hut provided for the shelter of shipwrecked sailors. He and Channing peered in through a knothole in the side of the tiny emergency shelter, "knowing that, though to him that knocketh it may not always be opened, yet to him that looketh long enough through a knot-hole, the inside shall be visible. . . ."

But the inside of the little hut revealed none of the required matches or kindling for a fire, not even a bench. "We thus looked through the knot-hole into the Humane house," he reported, "and for bread we found a stone."

Thoreau considered the little hut a pathetic excuse for mercy and said so: "We thought how cold is charity! how inhumane humanity!"

In fact, the futile "Charity Houses" were soon to be replaced by a much more effective form of aid for distressed ships. By 1872, the first lifesaving stations were established along the Outer Cape, and the Cape Codders manning them heroically saved many lives. Their stern credo—"You have to go out, but you don't have to come back"—sent them in surf boats out through the churning waves to pluck many a hapless soul from many a crumbling deck.

Later, the lifesaving stations themselves were made unnecessary by modern electronics and the Cape Cod Canal, which routed northbound ships across the safer waters of Cape Cod Bay. By the 1930s the lifesaving stations were obsolete and had closed.

But at Cahoon Hollow, today's beach walker can—at least in the summer months—stop in for a more contemporary form of rescue at one of the former lifesaving stations. The old building has been converted into the Beachcomber, a pleasant restaurant and bar. There friendly waitresses will bring the weary hiker a beer and a plate of Wellfleet oysters.

Thus the lifesaving station that Thoreau probably would have approved of (and which replaced the Charity House he scorned) has become one of the "bar-rooms of Massachusetts" that he so vigorously detested! Such are the changes time and fashion have wrought on the Outer Cape.

— — —

From Cahoon Hollow, a walk of a little over a mile northward brings the traveler to Newcomb Hollow, where, in 1849, Thoreau and Channing turned off the near-deserted beach and walked inland, looking for a place to spend the night. They were probably the first actual tourists on the Cape. Travelers there were so unusual in 1849 that people thought the two might be bank robbers.

It was customary then for travelers in rural areas to seek lodging in private homes and, within a half-mile from the beach, the two men found a family that would take them in—the family of John Newcomb, immortalized by Thoreau as "The Wellfleet Oysterman" in one of the most lively and entertaining chapters of *Cape Cod*. After some initial questioning, old John Newcomb let the two travelers in. His elderly wife fed them supper and then Newcomb (never named in the book) proceeded to regale them with a lively evening of stories and conversation. The family consisted of the old man and his wife, an elderly daughter, a mentally deficient older son, and a small boy of about ten. Channing talked with the women and Thoreau with the old man, who took center stage as the narrative continued.

"This was the merriest old man that we had ever seen, and one of the best preserved," Thoreau wrote. "His conversation was coarse and plain enough to have suited Rabelais."

At eighty-eight, Newcomb was still engaged in oyster farming; Thoreau first guessed that he might be considerably younger, in his sixties or seventies. But Newcomb declared, "I am a poor, good-for-nothing crittur, as Isaiah says; I am all broken down this year."

After an evening of banter and stories, the two visitors were locked into their bedroom—just to be on the safe side! And in the morning, Newcomb entertained them further, talking away while standing in front of the fireplace where a breakfast of buttermilk cake, eels, green beans, doughnuts, and tea warmed on the coals. Newcomb was chewing tobacco as he talked, spitting into the fireplace behind him without looking.

"I ate of the applesauce and doughnuts, which I thought had sustained the least detriment from the old man's shots, but my companion refused the apple-sauce, and ate of the hot cake and green beans, which had appeared to him to occupy the safest part of the hearth," Thoreau wrote. "But on comparing notes afterward, I told him that the buttermilk cake was particularly exposed, and I saw how it suffered repeatedly, and therefore I avoided it; but he declared that however that might be, he witnessed that the apple-sauce was seriously injured, and had therefore declined that."

After some more jesting and stories, Channing and Thoreau took their leave of the old man and started again walking northward along the beach. It was their second morning on the Cape.

John Newcomb is buried, along with other members of his family, in Wellfleet's Duck Creek Cemetery. His stone, sadly, is broken in two. His house still stands on the brow of a small hill northeast of Williams Pond, not far from the hollow and public beach that bears his name. The house has been painted white and added onto. Yet even with the changes, it is still identifiable by its idiosyncratic scattering of windows, which Thoreau described and which show up in old photographs. The house is privately owned. To visit a similar Cape Cod house that is publicly owned, contact the Cape Cod National Seashore, which has tours and other programs at the 18th-century Atwoods-Higgins House in Wellfleet during the warmer months.

The social and environmental changes that have transformed the Cape are vividly evident as you walk in the Newcomb Hollow area. The open hills of 1849, like most of the rest of the Cape, are now completely forested. Open heathland, such as Thoreau and Channing walked over to approach the Newcomb family home, is now a relatively rare habitat. Newcomb pointed out to Thoreau the seven ponds visible from his home, but most of them are now masked by the woods.

Thoreau predicted that the Cape would one day become "a place of resort" for the rest of New England. But he could not have foreseen how completely tourism has transformed the American economy and the land itself. As you walk along "Thoreau Way," the pervasive culture of today's leisure and recreation economy can be glimpsed through the trees in the dozens of well-tended vacation homes and the ever-present "No Trespassing" and "Private Way" signs alongside the thin, sandy trace of public road.

Most of the wild Cape has been tamed. The ravaged, sandy hills through which Thoreau and Channing walked are now forested and stabilized. That is the good news. However, where they are not publicly owned, more often than not, they have been subdivided and built upon. Only the establishment of the Cape Cod National Seashore in 1961 saved the lower Cape and the great Outer Beach from destruction by development. Even so, much of the Cape has become private and inaccessible. Without the protection of the National Seashore, the traffic of commerce that Thoreau despised would have triumphed completely.

One look at a detailed map makes this clear. Within the boundaries of the National Seashore, open lands still prevail. Outside those boundaries (and the boundaries of other, smaller nature preserves) a latticelike grid of roads and driveways covers the land nearly everywhere.

Like much of rural New England, the Cape has been developed and transformed. Cape Cod naturalist and writer Robert Finch notes in his fine book *A Place Apart* that the Cape's year-round population in the fifty years from 1940 to 1990 grew from about 30,000 people to more than 175,000. It is now almost 250,000, and summer visitors swell the ranks to more than a half-million. Finch notes that as momentous as the physical changes those numbers suggest may be, the social, environmental, and, if you will, spiritual changes are perhaps even more profound.

"Change, and an accompanying sense of loss, form perhaps the dominant strain in contemporary Cape Cod literature," he writes.

The "bar-rooms of Massachusetts"—and the restaurants, art galleries, souvenir shops, clam shacks, and stores selling trinkets, liquor, clothing, boats, hardware, "gifts," groceries, T-shirts, taffy, and inflatable toys—now dominate the Cape scene. They are always busy in the summer. Many people spend their vacation days wandering through them shopping, and miss the wild beauty of the place itself.

~ ~ ~

Yet despite the enormous changes that have transformed the Cape, glimpses—and more than glimpses, great panoramas—of its profound, timeless beauty remain. That is still a large part of what draws people there. North from Newcomb Hollow, the Great Beach is still beautiful, still mostly unspoiled, still very much a place apart.

And for most of the year, the long-distance walker there still walks alone. From fall through spring—nine months of the year—the sight of others on vast stretches of the Outer Beach is a rarity. Perhaps a few fishermen, a cruising SUV or two, but very few people walking, September through May.

True, in summer there may be thousands of people scattered along the sands at designated public "beaches." Such "beaches" exist wherever a parking area and a paved road meet the shore. There are about a dozen such points—roads and parking lots—in the twenty-eight miles between Nauset Harbor and Race Point.

And at each of them on sunny summer days, an alluvial fan of humanity deposits itself along the sandy shore and bakes in the sun. The beautiful bodies of young people, the less beautiful bodies of the rest of us, playing, dozing, arrayed on colorful beach towels, under colorful umbrellas, offering up a profusion of recorded music and assorted radio noise, flying frisbees and volleyballs, the smell of hot coconut oil.

And yet most of the Great Beach is virtually unpopulated, even in summer. Ten minutes of walking and you're past the latest outcropping of suntan lotion and electronic chatter and swallowed up once more in the great rhythmic silences of sand and ocean.

Once, walking the Outer Beach, I came upon a nude beach. There was a merry bare-assed game of volleyball underway (fascinating!) and occasionally one of the bolder members of the tribe would stroll casually down to the water's edge to splash some cooling water on, or possibly just for display purposes. That was the moment I came to one of my minor epiphanies: clothes have a purpose—naked, we are not a beautiful species. Most of us aren't, anyway.

A Coast Guard seaplane went by, its winglights (and probably its occupants' eyes) bulging and blinking cheerfully. I walked on, and the airplane turned and made another pass along the beach. As I trudged around the next point of shore, it was making its third sortie.

And then I was back in the simplicity of beach and ocean, sandy bluff and overarching sky. To the right, the bright green waters near the shore, then the deeper blue waters offshore, and, far away, near the gently curving horizon, the hints of ultramarine and purple. Directly ahead, the light tans of the beach. To the left, the bluff-face rose in layers of ocher, red, and darker tans, topped every now and then with a thatch of green. Land and ocean were separated only by a constant flashing skein of white surf, growling and slapping rhythmically along the shore.

This elemental configuration of land and sea remains essentially the same for mile after mile, hour after hour, as you walk. After a while, the constantly evaluating natter of inner dialogue that passes for mind begins to shut down. And then you are simply walking, moving calmly through a wide, pulsating, sunlit world. Despite the physical sameness of the landscape—the bank, the beach, the ocean—it never grows repetitive or boring. It is inviting, alive, and hypnotic. On my walks I rarely met a single soul—until I once again approached a road, a parking lot, a "beach."

Truth to tell, often when I climbed the bluff and looked inland, I could see vacation homes and roads and traffic glinting in the sunlight.

The Great Beach is a world apart, but not that far apart from the Great Beast. Yet something of its primordial wildness still lives.

There are still wild birds in profusion: cliff swallows, bank and rough-winged swallows, all swooping from their nest-holes in the banks, scooping up insects. Various plovers and sandpipers patter along at the edge of the surf, looking slightly mechanical, like small, exquisitely fashioned wind-up toys. And in the early summer, there are tern colonies, nesting—common terns, least terns, and, more rarely, roseate and arctic terns.

For obvious reasons, the terns prefer remote parts of the beach. Terns, like other manifestations of wildness, are threatened by humanity's growing pressure. Rolling SUVs can devastate their shallow nests in the sand, and too much attention from hikers or swimmers stirs up the adults and can expose the young in the nests to sun or predacious gulls. So the National Seashore puts up protective signs and urges everyone to leave the terns alone. The birds themselves fiercely encourage such an attitude, I found out on more than one walk.

My first incursion on their turf was my initiation. As I approached a fenced-in nesting area, the graceful, sickle-winged birds began boiling into the sky, complaining in harsh, shrill cries. One tern flew fairly close, and then hovered momentarily above me. I stopped walking and looked up, admiring its neat plumage and precise grace.

"Hi," I said, idiotically.

The bird instantly tilted downward and dived directly toward my eyes.

I ducked, the bird shot over my head and out to sea, did a perfect Immelmann turn, and returned for another pass. Up ahead dozens more of his tern allies were swarming into the sky.

I clamped my hat farther down over my head and began waving my bandanna at my assailants and shouting as I walked briskly along. I stayed as far from the terns' nests as possible, sometimes walking at the surf's edge and sometimes walking right in the surf, all the while assuring them at the top of my lungs that I had never owned a dune buggy or even a sand shovel. But the birds clearly didn't understand my language or trust my intentions. They continued to buzz me, squeaking, sometimes at star-tlingly close range, until I was well beyond their colony. Thoreau noted their shrill cries and active defense of their nests in the 19th century, and observed them driving larger birds clear across the Cape. He liked them.

After I had passed a couple more of their nesting colonies, I realized that the terns, small and fiercely comic as they might be, had conve-niently provided me with just that quality I had been seeking: wildness. They didn't care at all about my nationality, skin color, morality, lan-guage, or good intentions. They just wanted me to get away from their nests, and were willing to throw their entire feathered beings into the defense. They were as remote as the sea, and as unforgiving. They could never be tamed or trained.

And I had to admit that for that first moment, they had truly fright-ened me. At last, there was the wildness Thoreau had promised along the Outer Beach and at the first tiny taste of it, I had, however slightly, turned away.

Of course, Thoreau had also balked perceptibly, when he met wild-ness, hairy and panting, on Katahdin in Maine, where he found himself a long way from his friends in Concord and wildness in the abstract. Thoreau's later, more balanced idea of wildness and nature stemmed in part from the profound shock he received in the fog on Katahdin's stony, unforgiving slopes. He eventually came to realize that humanity appre-ciates wildness best from an enclave of order; that we need wilderness, but we can't live there.

It may have seemed to Thoreau that on Cape Cod, he had found civilization and wildness in proper balance. He could stand on the beach and imagine the storm wrecking ships and drowning people. He could see the colors of the ocean change from moment to moment, watch the tides come and go and feel the eternity of sameness amongst them. And then he could retire to a fisherman's cabin or a lighthouse for shelter and chat with the witty, resilient country people he found there.

It became an ideal landscape for his ruminations, and he returned to it several times. Channing, his frequent companion, declared that

Thoreau loved Cape Cod, and there seems little reason to doubt it. It is an easy place to fall in love with, even today.

— — —

Thoreau continued his walk northward. He stayed overnight at the Highland Light, then walked across the barren Cape to North Truro. Then he went on into Provincetown.

The bluff he walked on for most of his journey northward reaches its greatest height in North Truro, where the Highland Light stands. There it is roughly 150 feet tall, and the ocher sands are mixed with great swaths of gray clay. Not far beyond, the northbound hiker passes Head of the Meadow Beach, where an extensive salt meadow lies pinioned between the northernmost reaches of the glacial bluff and the ocean.

And then at High Head, the towering bluff ends, the Province Lands begin, and the character of the land subtly changes. High Head is the northernmost extension of the glacially deposited lands. North and west of that landmark lie the Province Lands, a lower, curving array of sand dunes, heather, salt-spray rose, and beach grass that was created by the wind and the sea. It forms the untamed "outback" behind Pilgrim Lake and Provincetown.

The Provincetown Thoreau walked into in 1849 was a rough fishing village with sandy streets four planks wide and codfish drying in front of nearly every house. He watched the hundreds of sails of the fishing fleet leave the harbor each day, round Race Point, and head out to sea.

"This was the most completely maritime town that we were ever in," he wrote, describing it as "an inhabited beach."

He enjoyed Provincetown. His writing continued to be high-spirited and humorous and he described how villagers "trundle out their fish and spread them in the morning, and bring them in at night." He describes the houses of Provincetown as literally surrounded by drying codfish with only a narrow path to the door remaining uncovered, "so that instead of looking out into a flower or grass plot, you looked on to so many square rods of cod turned wrong side outwards."

He saw houses with huge banks of sand drifted like snow against their outer walls and described an abandoned schoolhouse "filled with sand up to the tops of the desks."

One can only wonder what Thoreau would have made of today's Provincetown, jammed with tourists and artists in summer, a bastion of gay culture year-round. The "fish-flakes" around the houses have been replaced by flower gardens (the poet Stanley Kunitz tended one of them well into his 90s) and the downtown has become a riot of tourist commerce, especially in the summer. Dozens of restaurants, souvenir shops, clothing stores, and art galleries jostle together on Commercial Street to tempt the recreational shopper. We can be reasonably sure that Thoreau would have scorned them.

But what might he have made of the village's overt gayness—the obvious homosexuality of its strolling male and female couples, and the "meat rack"—the benches in front of Town Hall where available gays wait to be picked up?

Thoreau's sexuality, described by one writer as "indeterminate," remains a mystery. He was turned down after a brief romance by Ellen Sewall, and never courted another woman—though he probably had an idealistic crush on Lydian Emerson, the wife of his friend and mentor, Ralph Waldo. His closest friendships were with men. At least one scholar with whom I discussed this book is convinced that Thoreau was gay, though I strongly doubt it. He was deeply in love with Ellen Sewall as a young man, and would almost certainly have married her, had her father not forbidden the match because of Thoreau's unconventional religious beliefs. On his deathbed, when someone mentioned Ellen's name, Thoreau murmured: "I have always loved her. I have always loved her." And there were other women he was attracted to, perhaps most notably the frankly sensual farm wife he encountered on the open slopes of Mount Greylock. In any case, we shall never really know.

Most likely, the glittery, casual, vigorously commercial Provincetown of the 21st century would simply be incomprehensible to him—far more foreign in his mind than the rough and exotic fishing village he actually visited. What we do know is that in 1849, Thoreau preferred the desolate wilderness of the Province Lands, the dunes, and the Great Beach. He noted that he and Channing saw mostly "the back side of the towns."

"We cannot say how its towns look in front to one who goes to meet them," he wrote. "We went to see the ocean behind them."

The Province Lands are now part of the Cape Cod National Seashore. Though Provincetown itself backs right up against them, their wild character is protected against development. However, even here, there are primitive roads and evidence of humanity.

On a recent October hike there, two friends and I trudged through a series of immense, sandy bowls following the winding jeep roads as they led us through clumps of scrub oak, swatches of bearberry and bog cranberry, with the pounding surf grumbling in our ears. It rained all day, but we had rain jackets and warm clothing and walked happily along. We threaded our way through the dune shacks, where writers and artists including Norman Mailer and Eugene O'Neill had summered and pursued their craft. The shacks are tiny inholdings within the park lands and presumably will be gradually eliminated, even though they, too, are a part of the Cape's cultural heritage.

When we climbed the final wall of dunes and looked out over the heaving gray sea, the surf's grumbling became a wild roar. We puttered our way northwestward, walked past the tumbled stone blocks that mark the site of the Peaked Hill Bars Rescue Station, and ate our sandwiches out of the weather, in a tiny grove of scrub oak that sheltered a depression among the dunes.

Then we clambered over more sandy hills, passed a lone tour jeep ("Happy Christmas!" yelled an exuberant Englishman from the window as the jeep rolled past us) and continued following the road's bare, sandy trace until we came to a broad, marshy plain, where shallow pools of water rippled off several hundred yards in every direction and heathery shrubs—bog cranberry, leatherleaf, bearberry, and sheep laurel—shivered in the constant wind.

Along one edge of this watery plain a huge flock of rough-winged swallows sat resting. Were they resident birds, flocking up in anticipation of their long flight south? Had they been blown in from the stormy ocean? Or had they become confused and blundered from the mainland out to this spit of sand? Such mysteries are among the pleasures of walking in an untamed landscape. For whatever reason, they now sat beside one of the larger pools of water, all facing eastward into the wind. They sat tight as we approached, but gradually one handful of birds would erupt into the air and disappear over the nearest wall of dunes, then another. And finally they all flew off, leaving us to speculate on their origin and the reason for the huge flock—probably more than a thousand birds—being there.

We had been walking several hours in the heavy, wet sand and were becoming tired. We threaded through a notch in the seaward wall of dunes, aiming to walk due west up the beach to Race Point and Provincetown.

"Look out," Mary yelled as I stumbled down onto the beach. One of the ever-present SUVs nearly nailed me. I stopped in time, and watched it roll past without slowing down, its windows rolled tightly up.

As we walked the final mile to Race Point, I could see the surf breaking over the once-deadly outer bars, white and angry-looking against the gray sky.

— — —

A ten-minute drive south of Provincetown, and a vast view of the ocean awaits from atop the bluff at Highland Light. Thoreau stayed at the earlier, original light on two of his journeys and lodged at the nearby Highland House on another. The old hotel has since been replaced by a building erected in 1907 which now houses the Truro Historical Society Museum, and the lighthouse was moved back from the edge of the crumbling bluff in 1996. It has been supplanted by modern electronics and the Cape Cod Canal, and is no longer used as a navigational aid. It is now a piece of the Cape's history, and sits on the outer edge of the Highland Links Golf Course. You now walk a graveled road through the golf course to get to the light. Beyond the light, a path leads to the edge of the bluff and a viewing platform.

It is mildly difficult to connect with Thoreau as you stand on the wooden platform with small electric carts toodling across the fairways behind you. Yet if you go there in the fall, as Thoreau suggested, the light will be eloquent, and after a storm the ocean will be lashed into frothy white surf for a quarter-mile offshore. Northern gannets and white-winged scoters and loons and grebes can often be seen diving into the surf, and a feeling of wild freedom prevails, despite the tamed landscape.

You never leave America, of course. We are, after all, standing on the edge of a golf course. Even on the Outer Beach, with the high glacial bluff's clifflike face blocking out the ruling clutter, one is seldom far from a rolling SUV equipped with a disk player and cup holder and fishing rods. But we are also on the edge of an absolute wilderness, the fierce Atlantic, that growls and slaps the shore. The connection with the Cape that Thoreau knew is tenuous and complex, but it is real.

The Cape today is a compromised landscape, as it was—for different reasons—in Thoreau's time. Its sands are no longer blowing wholesale into the sea, but its aquifers are endangered by excessive development. Economically prosperous, it is overrun with cars and people for four months, and quieter the rest of the year.

It is both whole and broken. It is a complex landscape, layered by time and change and the ironies of time and change. It is all there—complete wildness, the great ocean; and inland our man-made tameness—our relentless commercial culture, our social problems and excesses, a fragile and challenged environment, beach heather, pitch pines, the preserved tracts of the National Seashore, the mute testimony of foxes, terns, bobwhites, and gulls.

We can see its interwoven complexity more clearly because it is so small, such a narrow strip of sand thrust out into the broad Atlantic. The complexity of our American life contrasts sharply with the beauty and simplicity of the wild beach and wilder ocean—all rendered compact and essential by this very small place.

And there is something more, too, something very difficult to define. You feel it when you stand on the windy bluff and look out beyond the trembling beach grass, beyond the foaming white surf, to the blue and green and (sometimes) purple ocean. And that is our deep human need for the elemental beauty this place possesses. We can't buy it or build it—we can only appreciate it, or destroy it. Thank whatever gods you choose—and the National Park Service—that timeless beauty is still there to be appreciated.

I think that the top of Mount Washington should not be private property; it should be left unappropriated for modesty and reverence's sake, or if only to suggest that earth has higher uses than we put her to.

—Journal, January 3, 1861

8

Mount Washington, Two Times

Today's Mount Washington is a paradox—a huge, wild mountain capped by a train station, a parking lot, and a hodgepodge of commercial and scientific development. The summit of the highest peak in New England is grotesquely overdeveloped.

Yet much of the mountain and the Presidential Range it dominates is as wild as it was in Thoreau's day. Washington is the culminating central peak of the Presidential Range, which includes eight or ten of the highest mountains in New England. Into the flanks of this range are carved spectacularly deep ravines. Old-growth forests rich in rare plants and wildlife clothe its lower flanks and, above treeline, the mountain is surrounded by the largest arctic-alpine meadow in New England, which extends for miles. A half-dozen streams cascade down its rocky sides, splashing their way into the Cutler, Pemigewasset, and Ammonoosuc watersheds. Washington and the Presidential Range constitute one of the Northeast's most important wild enclaves, overlooking the long-tamed landscape below: the highways, villages, farms, and tourist amenities of northern New England.

It is 6,288 feet high, small by world standards. Yet because of its northern location and height, it attracts wild, often deadly weather. The signs at treeline warning that hikers have died on the meadows above in every month of the year are soberingly accurate.

All of which makes the commercial melange on the summit of Mount Washington even stranger, by contrast. It is the fate of "highest" peaks to be mercilessly popular, and Mount Washington is an extreme example of the result. An auto road and a cog railroad regularly deliver gangs of tourists to the summit. The hulking, concrete Sherman Adams Summit Building, Mussolini-modern in style, houses the offices and equipment of the Mount Washington Observatory and also serves as a tourist center, complete with cafeteria, restrooms, and gift shops. An assorted collection of telecommunication towers, railroad tracks, pipes and cables, parking lots and cars almost completely covers the highest point in New England.

Tourists who ride the cog railroad or drive up the auto road may emerge to find themselves in rain, cold winds, or impenetrable fog—true mountain weather. Hikers who have toiled up through rocky ravines and wind-whipped alpine slopes finally approach the summit through crammed parking lots, wooden stairways, and a maze of wandering pipes and telecom cables. The fifty-nine-acre Mount Washington State Park probably devotes a higher percentage of its surface area to concrete and pavement than any other park in New Hampshire.

From afar, this array looks like a futuristic space station perched on the mountaintop: Star Wars come to the Presidential Range. But up close, as the trainloads and carloads of tourists come and go, it feels more like a second-rate, crowd-worn bus station. We can be sure that Thoreau would have hated it, because he saw its beginnings and hated them.

Thoreau climbed Mount Washington twice, in 1839 and again nineteen years later, in 1858.

We know almost nothing about his first climb because he wrote almost nothing about it. We do know that it was in September of 1839, Thoreau was twenty-two years old, and he was with his brother, John.

We also know that he was climbing a wilderness peak. The summit of Mount Washington in 1839 was almost completely pristine. There were no buildings atop it, and only primitive trails led there.

The hike was the climax of the river journey the two young men made together, the journey that Thoreau immortalized in his first book, *A Week on the Concord and Merrimack Rivers*. It is a long, discursive book, full of details, side trips, and intellectual digressions. But the episode that might well have been its climax, his climb to the summit of Mount Washington, is presented only in a brief, vague account, less than a single sentence out of a book nearly four hundred pages long. Thoreau's main interest apparently lay in tracing the river to its source and in memorializing his brother, who died tragically in 1842 of tetanus. The mountain climb that was the culmination of their trip seems almost an afterthought as he describes it. He uses the Indian name for the mountain, Agiocochook, possibly to mythologize the mountain and the climb:

"Thus, in fair days as well as foul, we had traced up the river to which our native stream is a tributary, until from the Merrimack it became the Pemigewasset that leaped by our side, and when we had passed its fountainhead, the Wild Amonoosuck, whose puny channel was crossed at a stride, guiding us toward its distant source among the mountains, and at length, without its guidance, we were enabled to reach the summit of Agiocochook."

And that's about it. Thoreau gives more space to a nervous young soldier that he and John encountered on the way to the mountains and to the purchase of a watermelon on the way back than he does to his first ascent of New England's highest peak! His journal entry for the day of the climb, September 10, 1839, is equally laconic.

"Ascended the mountain and rode to Conway," he notes. End of story.

Quite uncharacteristically, he gives us no information about his route up the mountain or what he saw there. From his brief journal entries, we know that the two Thoreaus stayed "at Crawford's" the night before their hike, so their most likely route up the mountain was

Crawford Path, the trail Abel and Ethan Allen Crawford had pioneered up the Presidential Range to Washington's summit in 1819. It's also a likely guess that the two brothers returned to Crawford House via the same path and were taken "to Conway" for the night by a Crawford wagon, horse-drawn.

What could Thoreau have told us about the summit? What did he see and experience? Was the day clear, the view brilliant and far-reaching? Or was the mountaintop wrapped in fog and mystery?

Unfortunately, he doesn't let us in on it. We are left with a puzzling void surrounding the young Thoreau's first significant mountain climb.

The first of the mountaintop structures was built two years after Thoreau and John visited there, and more have followed, relentlessly.

However, much of the surrounding mountain landscape remains unchanged. Though Crawford Path has been slightly re-routed over the intervening century and a half, it is still the main route from Crawford Notch over the Southern Presidentials to Mount Washington. And it still passes through a wild, open, often unforgiving swath of mountain-top terrain.

The range is a massive granite ridge running roughly north-south in the midst of northern New Hampshire's White Mountains. It is the largest single range of mountains in New England, much of it more than five thousand feet high, a huge portion of it thrusting above treeline. It is roughly eleven miles long. Mount Washington is the centerpiece of this broad, stony upland. Its immense bulk rises a thousand feet above the rest of the range and dominates it from every angle.

To the north, New England's three next highest mountains surround a spectacularly deep glacial ravine, the Great Gulf, in a striking display of mountain grandeur. They are mounts Adams, Jefferson, and Madison, all more than five thousand feet high. To the south, the castlelike Mount Monroe, the broad shoulder of Mount Franklin, and the great rounded dome of Mount Eisenhower loom above a wide alpine meadow. On all sides, other lesser mountains are arrayed, range after range, off into the far, blue distance.

It is a craggy, rock-bound spectacle, utterly unlike the neat villages and quiet pastoral scenes normally associated with New England. Its wild landscape would have been utterly new to the young Thoreau and can still move visitors deeply today. Yet perhaps even more striking than the dramatic grandeur of the Presidential Range is its profound beauty. Once it rises above timberline, just north of Mount Clinton, the Crawford Path meanders upward through the largest alpine meadow in New England, a rolling upland where fields of tawny deer's-hair sedge, tiny bog cranberry, bearberry, diapensia, Lapland rosebay, and alpine azalea gradually supplant patches of weather-stunted spruce and fir as the trail winds higher and higher.

The distant views—range upon range of blue mountains over green valleys—reach to the horizon, while at the hiker's feet, heath shrubs and tiny plants group themselves into small, exquisite garden-like arrangements. Washington looms above, and on sunny days in summer and early fall, a hiker climbing ever-higher through this windswept, heathy meadow feels as exhilarated and free as the mountain landscape through which he walks.

This was, in fact, the mountain landscape through which Henry and John Thoreau walked on September 10, 1839. And Thoreau, America's first great naturalist writer, wrote almost nothing about it. The question is: why?

No answer is completely satisfactory. It could be that he omitted any description of the spectacular scene for literary reasons. *A Week on the Concord and Merrimack Rivers* was, after all, explicitly about a river trip. The book was written, at least in part, as a tribute and memorial to John Thoreau, the brother whom Henry treasured dearly, probably the closest friend he ever had. It has been suggested that by using the Native American name for the mountain, Agiocochook ("Home of the Great Spirit"), and by keeping the details of the climb vague, Thoreau may have felt he was personally conducting his brother to heaven.

Or something like that.

It is, at best, a weak explanation. It may be simply that Thoreau declined to describe the view from the summit because he couldn't see it. Mount Washington and the Presidentials are wrapped in clouds about three-fourths of the time. Thoreau's journal for September 9 (the day before the climb) notes only that he spent the day "At Crawford's." He didn't take rest days. Most likely he and John were waiting out inclement weather. On September 10, they climbed the mountain, returned, and proceeded by wagon to Conway. Perhaps they climbed the mountain in fog, after a day of waiting out the rain. No view to see; no view to describe.

A third possibility is that Thoreau ignored the glorious view on purpose—that he was indulging his disdain for the Romantic, gushing descriptions of mountain scenery then becoming popular. But all we can do is speculate.

And Thoreau doesn't give us any help on the matter at all.

***

The alpine meadows of the Presidential Range are not only exceptionally beautiful. They can be exceptionally dangerous as well. More than a hundred people have died there, some even in summer. Though the alpine zone can seem placid and parklike on a calm summer day, its high altitude and exposure to the sudden, furious storms of northern New England can turn it deadly in minutes.

I had this grim history vividly in mind on an autumn climb over the Southern Presidentials to Washington not long ago. I had no desire to die of hypothermia, but it did seem at least a theoretical possibility that day.

I was hiking with Scott Skinner, my hiking companion for many years, and Walter Jones, his friend. Walter desperately wanted to climb the mountain, but his bad knees would never survive the long trudge down from the summit, so a complicated hiking plan had been cooked up: Walter's cheerful wife, Peggy, would drop us off at the Edmands Path, which we would then climb to the ridgetop near Mount Eisenhower. We would meet Crawford Path there and follow it to the summit of Mount Washington. Walter's knees, like most knees, work fine uphill, and he's plenty fit. So barring mishaps, he would summit, with Scott and me in tow. Peggy, meanwhile, would drive around to Pinkham Notch and up the Mount Washington Auto Road, meeting us at the top. At that point we would all swallow our pride and ride down the auto road with Peggy. Not a very Thoreauvian plan, but it would allow Walter to climb Washington, and it would give all of us a good hike and the pleasure of walking through the great alpine meadow of the Presidentials.

Or at least that's what we thought, until we met Walter at the Mount Washington Hotel and saw the Presidential Range completely hooded in ominous-looking black clouds. Quiet reigned in the car as we drove to Edmands Path. Peggy, wearing a broad-brimmed orange straw hat and chatting happily with Scott, walked up the trail with us for a ways. Then she turned back to do her drive-around and meet us at the summit train station.

Edmands Path is sheltered in the trees until it reaches the little col between mounts Eisenhower and Franklin. That is precisely where we emerged into the open area above treeline, and precisely where the weakness in our plan became clear.

The dark, ominous clouds were still present; they wrapped the mountains above us in a soggy, opaque cloak. A cold wind was ripping harshly through the col. We were all sweating from the climb, but the wind quickly put an end to that. Suddenly we were damp and chilled. We bustled into parkas and sweaters and wind pants, plus the most important piece of gear for me and my bald head—a wool cap!

Even with the extra clothing, I was nervously aware that we were entering perfect hypothermia conditions on a dangerous open mountain ridge. I wolfed down a sandwich to quell my anxiety. It sat in my stomach like a brick.

We could turn back, I suggested. But Scott, bless him, would have none of it. Peggy's going to be on top of the mountain waiting for us, he pointed out. So we've got to go. (Translation in my mind: we're doomed.)

There was a bit of hope. The sky was lighter off to the west; and bits of blue sky gleamed hopefully between the ranks of clouds marching toward us. Well, I thought, might as well get walking. It's only a couple of easy miles to the Lakes of the Clouds Hut. We can hole up there if it's really bad.

As I was rearranging my pack and pulling on my wind pants, three shadowy forms scampered across the col and climbed into the mists swathing Mount Franklin. Had I imagined them? By the time I had re-shouldered my pack, Scott and Walter had disappeared.

Great. Rule One of hiking in restricted visibility is not to get separated from your party and I had just broken it. "Walter!" I began shouting. "Scott!"

Suddenly there they were, sheltered in a rocky nook below me. I hustled down to rejoin them. "Are you all right?" Walter immediately asked, obviously worried that I had lost my mind. I assured him I was fine—just concerned that I had somehow misplaced them. And so the hike continued.

Then one of those minor miracles that justify all the sweat and pain of long uphill trudges occurred. Almost as soon as we began walking, the clouds began to lift. As we climbed higher up Franklin, the wind, instead of increasing, abated slightly. We headed north along Crawford Path, picking our way up Franklin's south slope, noticing other hikers far above us doing the same. We clambered up and over the tawny brown ridge as the wind whipped the lingering shreds of cloud off the top and flung them off to the east—where, miraculously, they disappeared.

The sky to the east had become a clear blue. Away on the western horizon, under the still-threatening sky, we could make out the long line of the Green Mountains, the familiar shapes of Mansfield and Camel's Hump. We topped out on Franklin's broad ridge and began walking toward the jagged fortress-like peaks of Mount Monroe and, farther beyond, the immense bulk of Washington, which was still wrapped in gray clouds.

We followed the Crawford Path through a rocky expanse of red-brown rushes and sedges that shook and trembled in the brisk wind. As we approached Monroe, we met three old wanderers (like us!) resting in a rocky enclave, using their huge backpacks for shelter from the chilly blast. They must have been the three shadowy forms that had passed us in the col. They turned out to be Kentuckians, retired postal workers who had hiked the entire Appalachian Trail in sections in the 1980s and 90s, and had come back to re-hike the most interesting sections again. They were dressed in the universal insulated ragtag common to all hikers above treeline this time of year and each of them sported a huge, woolly touque.

They spoke in soft Southern drawls: "We ded this part about this tahm nine yurs ago," said the one with the neatly trimmed white moustache. "But ah don't remember thur bein' so much up-hiyull." Yup, we answered (undoubtedly in what the Kentuckians identified as a clipped Northern accent), there is a lot of uphill in this section.

Walter, summit lust glittering in his eyes, decided at that point to climb over Monroe to the hut, and Scott volunteered to go with him. I've climbed Monroe a dozen times, and wanted to save my legs for Washington. I opted for the easier walk around Monroe and stayed on Crawford Path as it wandered through patches of krummholz (stunted fir trees), and open sections of alpine meadow emblazoned with heath shrubs and rare arctic-alpine plants. Just before Lakes of the Clouds Hut, there's a portion of the trail that is carefully fenced in to protect the extremely rare dwarf cinquefoil. The plant is found nowhere else in the United States.

Our hike had turned from a survival epic into an enjoyable walk, and soon I was sitting comfortably on a bench outside the hut, soaking up the afternoon sunshine. I had glimpsed the three postmen (ret.) inside, leafing through old hut journals, looking for the entry they had made on their 1993 trip through the area.

As I sat there in the shelter of the hut's two ells, a yellow helicopter rose up from the valley below and came whacking in directly over the entryway. From its belly dangled a net bag of food and supplies. "Yayyy!" shouted one of the female members of the hut crew. "Toilet paper!"

It's pleasant to watch other people work. The youthful hut staff unloaded the supplies and the chopper whirred away. I sipped a cup of hot coffee, ate my remaining sandwich, and watched Scott and Walter pick their way down from the summit of Mount Monroe. After some more food and a few minutes' rest, we pressed on. The clouds by then had completely lifted off Mount Washington and its sun-dappled flanks were calling us—time to get up there!

We clambered upward on the stones of Crawford Path, ascending gradually at first, then more steeply as the path slabbed across and up, back and forth, zigzagging up the steep summit cone. It's hard to imagine horses making this climb, but they used to, a hundred and more years ago. A thin, towheaded girl from the hut crew blasted past us with no apparent effort, even though she was burdened with a big pack frame. Soon she was above us and completely out of sight. Looking back and down we could see we were above the summit of Monroe, so we stopped occasionally to rest and soak up the long, brooding, autumnal views. Not too many more days before fall and winter storms would close these mountains down to all but the boldest.

A few more minutes climbing and we could see the stunning array of Northern Peaks over Washington's shoulder. And then, suddenly, we were approaching the summit—and the outworks of civilization: railroad tracks, propane tanks, communications cables, towers, wandering tourists, parking lots, directional signs. We picked our way through all this, climbed some wooden stairs, and stood on the very summit of Mount Washington. There was no view. We were completely surrounded by buildings.

At least one earlier writer claimed that the view from Washington was disappointing. The mountain is so high, the view so distant, went this opinion, that it loses impact. If true, that has certainly been fixed by the current situation. Now, standing next to the historic Tip Top House, surrounded by towers and buildings and signs, you can't see the view at all.

At least not from the actual summit. The Northern Presidentials remain one of the great and most magnificent landscapes of New England—a symphony of huge, stony peaks and deep ravines. The views of them from Mount Washington are grand in every sense of the word. But you have to step away from the congestion on the peak to see them.

— — —

Nineteen years after his first hike up Mount Washington, Thoreau came back. By July of 1858, both he and the mountain had changed.

He was forty-one years old, had established himself as a writer, and acquired a consuming interest in field botany, plus a life's mission of reforming humanity. Though middle aged, he was physically very strong, and at the height of his powers as a writer.

In the years between his two trips to Mount Washington, American society had undergone one of its great sea changes. The Romantic rage for sublimity had flowered in America. Mountains, which had been regarded as inconvenient, often-dangerous impediments to travel and progress, had been transformed in the public consciousness into fashionable tourist destinations. Mountain journeys had become equated with the search for God-in-nature, and every cultured person longed to go climbing in them—or at least go on a vacation where one could spend time looking at them.

This urge, carefully cultivated by promoters and developers, brought tourists to the White Mountains by train and carriage-load. Since Thoreau's last visit, Mount Washington had acquired several more trails, two summit houses, a partially completed carriage road, and a tourist clientele.

Thoreau studiously ignored all of that and concentrated instead on his botanizing. In a lengthy series of journal entries, he described his trip from Concord to the summit of Mount Washington in scrupulous, almost obsessive detail, telling us where he and his companions camped, the routes he followed on and off the mountain, virtually every plant he encountered, birds he saw and heard, even the compass bearings of some of his best views. The contrast with that earlier vague, one-sentence account of his trip up the Crawford Path couldn't be more pronounced.

He had been invited to go and botanize on Mount Washington by his friend, the Concord attorney Edward Hoar. When Thoreau said he wasn't sure whether he could afford the trip, Hoar said he would hire a horse and wagon and the trip wouldn't cost Thoreau anything. Thoreau agreed, though with characteristic grumpiness, he was soon complaining that traveling by horse and wagon made everything unpleasantly complicated.

"It is far more independent to travel on foot. You have to sacrifice so much to the horse," he groused in his journal. The horse's annoying need for food and water meant that the best places for lunch stops and campsites—Thoreau meant those with nice views—had to be passed by. "The only alternative is to spend your noon at some trivial inn, pestered by flies and tavern loungers," he wrote.

They made their way northeastward across New Hampshire, passing lakes Squam and Winnipesaukee, where they spent a day climbing Red Hill and admired the flesh-colored rocky spire of Mount Chocorua. It took Thoreau and Hoar six days to travel from Concord to Pinkham Notch and the base of the half-finished carriage road (today's Mount Washington Toll Road). They sent the horse and carriage back down the notch, and began walking up the road toward the summit. With them was William H.H. Wentworth, whom Hoar had hired to help out. They were anticipating meeting two friends, Theo Brown and Harrison Blake, on the mountain, though little planning had been done regarding a rendezvous.

As he began climbing the mountain, Thoreau's botanical interests surged to the forefront and his journal began to bristle with Latin names. He noted the changes in the forest as he climbed—changes such as the shift from yellow birch and maple trees to spruce-fir forest that hikers can still see on New England's mountainsides. His party made arrangements to stay at a collier's shanty, near treeline on the road, where charcoal was made to heat the two summit houses. Thoreau noted that he went on alone above the shanty "and found many new Alpine plants," before returning for the night.

The following morning, he arose early and made his way alone above treeline and to the summit. He wanted to get ahead of the clouds that he was sure would soon obscure the view, and he was obviously excited by the chance to see and record the plants which had stirred his interest the day before.

In Thoreau's day, new and rare plants were still being discovered on the heights of the Presidentials. Serious botanists, in fact, were among the first explorers of the region above treeline; from about 1816 on, they regularly climbed to the alpine zone to study plants that could normally be seen only in the Arctic and other far northern regions. Many of the features of the range today are named after those early, pioneering botanists—Tuckerman and Huntington ravines, Bigelow Lawn, Oakes Gulf, and Boott Spur among them. A wave of talented amateur botanists, including Thoreau and Hoar, followed in the wake of those pioneer scientists.

By 1858, Thoreau's interest in botany had grown far beyond the hobbyist stage, and he had become quite expert—though he sometimes made mistakes, which subsequent generations of naturalists rarely fail to point out. Nevertheless, botany was the consuming interest of his later years, and he worked at it carefully and diligently during his 1858 trip to the White Mountains. He and Hoar had left Concord with a list of forty-six plants that they wished to see in the mountains. They found forty-two of them.

As he clambered up the mountain on July 8, ahead of his companions, he noted many alpine plants: bog bilberry, bearberry willow, diapensia, black crowberry, mountain cranberry, fir clubmoss, three-toothed cinquefoil, mountain avens, moss campion, and everywhere blooming the delicate white blossoms of the mountain sandwort. Hikers today still encounter these plants and still marvel at their delicate beauty.

Thoreau got to the summit in time for a quick, hazy view, but an enveloping cloud rolled in, wrapped the summit in mist, and obscured the view for the others. He got a look at the spectacular topography of the Northern Peaks, but confused their names, probably because of a faulty map he had traced on his way to the mountains.

Actually, he was more than confused. His journal indicates he was stubbornly wrong. He consistently called Mount Jefferson, the first major summit north of Washington, Mount Adams and vice versa. Even though a caretaker at the summit told him his map was wrong and that Adams was actually the second summit north of Washington, Thoreau persisted in switching the identities of the two mountains, also misnaming them several days later in a sketch he made of the Presidential Range from a hillside in the town of Jefferson.

But his skill in using his compass was undiminished and, despite the fog, Thoreau led his companions down the mountain accurately to Tuckerman Ravine by following a compass bearing he had taken from the summit before the clouds rolled in. Today, the Tuckerman Ravine Trail approximates Thoreau's route. It is marked with huge cairns and painted blazes to assist hikers. Even so, when mist envelops the mountain, hikers can still get lost and wander into dangerous areas.

It was at this moment that Thoreau's Mount Washington adventure began to turn bad. An objective observer today might describe Thoreau's journey through Tuckerman Ravine as semi-disastrous: he sprained his ankle in a fall, tore his fingernails in a desperate self-arrest on a snow slope, and a member of his party started a forest fire that blackened much of Boott Spur. But Thoreau didn't see it as a disaster. He remained undaunted and witty, the careful, fascinated observer, even though confined to camp for a day by his sprained ankle.

He continued identifying and cataloguing the plants he saw, observed a small owl that visited their camp one night (most likely a saw-whet owl), and described so precisely the call of an unseen bird that even amateur birders 150 years later know that he heard a winter wren, a tiny brown bird with a long, twittering song that is still a familiar companion in the mountains of northern New England.

When blackflies attacked—a common and unpleasant affliction in the White Mountains in July—Thoreau, ever the compleat Mr. Science, observed them carefully, and categorized them as they chewed his flesh. "The black flies, which pestered us till into evening, were of various sizes," he wrote with admirable detachment, "the largest more than an eighth of an inch long."

While Thoreau and his friends were camping in the ravine, a group of a hundred politicians and journalists had climbed to Mount Washington's summit to celebrate the building of the carriage road. The road wouldn't be complete for another two years, but that didn't stop the celebration. *Walden* was in print and Thoreau's essay on his Maine trip to Lake Chesuncook had just been published in the *Atlantic*, so he was known as an outdoorsman. A subsequent article in the *New York Tribune* referred to him as the "Concord Pan," and marveled that his party had been able to sleep warm and dry on a bed of boughs in their cotton tent.

"We could not help shivering, as we looked down the ravine the next morning and saw the banks of snow that are all but eternal, and the little black pools a mile below, beside which the party camped for four nights."

What did the group of dignitaries and journalists make of the black swath scorched on the mountainside by the party of the Concord Pan? One wonders.

The fire got its start when a campfire kindled by Wentworth got out of control. Near the Little Headwall the group had foolishly hacked a small clearing for their campsite out of the dense, stunted firs alongside the brook. Wentworth, who had been hired in Glen, New Hampshire, as a packer and camp steward, kindled his fire atop some dry moss on the lee side of the clearing. The moss ignited, the blaze spread to the nearby firs and raced up the mountainside, whipped along by a brisk wind.

Thoreau was careful to point out that he had counseled Wentworth to remove the moss before starting the fire, and noted that the party had to scramble to salvage their gear. Wentworth, however, was glib, saying the fire "would do no harm," and Thoreau, true to form, was soon speculating scientifically on the effects of fires in the mountains.

They made no attempt to put the runaway fire out. It burned to the top of the ridge and smoldered away until a steady rain two days later finally quenched it. When Blake and Brown caught up with Thoreau, he noted wryly, the still-smoldering fire on Boott Spur in mind:

"I had told Blake to look out for a smoke and a white tent, and we had made a smoke sure enough."

The next day, while exploring along the brook, Thoreau sprained his ankle. But even in distress, his wealth of practical knowledge served him well. Immediately after he fell, he plunged his foot into the icy brook that drains the ravine and wrapped his sprained ankle in arnica, a mountain flower with a bright yellow blossom known as an herbal remedy for pain and swelling. Although the pain kept him awake that night, after a day's rest he could walk again.

After another day of waiting out the rain, Thoreau and his companions hiked down to Pinkham Notch, recovered their wagon, and went north to Gorham, where they made camp. It was still raining as they camped again in Jefferson. But the weather cleared and, as Thoreau watched, a beautiful sunset colored the Presidentials. As the sun dappled the mountains, he made a sketch of the range and labeled the prominent peaks. Once again, he carefully, stubbornly misidentified Jefferson and Adams.

━ ━ ━

I knew I was in trouble as I watched Ed, our leader, slip out of his hiking boots and into special rock-climbing shoes. Hmmm. I didn't have rock-climbing shoes, just my worn, smooth-soled boots. We were in Huntington Ravine, at the Fan, a rock formation at the bottom of the serious steeps.

I had decided on this trail as an alternative to Thoreau's actual route—up the carriage road—because that is now the Mount Washington Auto Road, and I didn't want to inhale exhaust fumes for two hours. My choice might have been better. The Huntington Ravine Trail is the most difficult hiking trail in the White Mountains.

As I sat there, contemplating my fate, a group of young women—college age or younger—clambered up from the jumbled talus below. They laughed and chatted as they crossed the steep, slick-looking section just ahead of us. And then they disappeared onto the cliffs above. It was our turn.

Ed crossed the steep rock, resplendent in his soft-soled rock-climbing shoes. I followed him while Scott snapped my photo from behind on the last secure outcrop. Did I look as craven and clumsy as I felt? There was a small stream of water trickling down the slanted rock. Having fallen more than once on steep, wet rocks, I wanted no part of it. I reached the edge of a raised slab of rock, edged a few feet along until it looked scalable, got a leg up it and pried myself upwards. The rock was suddenly dry and more level. I could walk upright. Almost.

I carefully followed the blazes that led upward over ledge after ledge. No looking back or down—my heart was already pounding fast enough, and I could feel the large distances that opened out behind and below me. In a couple of places, smooth rock with barely a fingernail-hold confronted me. I shamelessly grabbed the roots and stunted trees alongside the bare slabs and pulled myself upwards, cursing my fate, my stupidity, my companions—whatever it was that had lured me into this desperate climb.

I made the mistake of looking up. A few hundred yards higher, a rocky parapet seemed to hang out over the near-vertical faces I was pulling myself awkwardly up. "How in hell," I thought, "am I ever going to get over that?" Teenaged female giggles floated down from above. The girls—the kids!—who had passed us were laughing as they made their way upward. Even though I couldn't see them, I was humbled. I kept climbing. At this point, retreat was not an option. Down was more dangerous than up.

I reached the upper corner of the hanging parapet, where I was confronted by a ledge that was slanted the wrong way—toward me—and was too high to climb over. I managed to get around it by crawling up a rough trough of bare rock on my hands and knees, which were already skinned raw.

And then, happily, the trail began to ease off. Its steepness abated and it became a series of giant, but manageable stairs. I didn't even have to use my hands. A final ledge and I stepped onto the upper lip of Huntington Ravine. Scott and Ed were sitting on rocks, pulling sweaters and sandwiches out of their packs. I looked at my watch. Noon! Somehow the morning had passed in an instant. I shuffled into a jacket and windpants and found the softest rock I could locate to eat lunch on.

Then we wandered across the broad plateau of the Alpine Garden, linked up with the Tuckerman Ravine Trail, and scrambled up the tumbled rocks of the summit cone. We had about five hundred feet to ascend to make the top. I knew we were getting close when I looked up and saw protruding out above me the underside of an SUV's chrome-plated grill. Civilization.

We climbed the wooden stairs that led upward through multiple parking lots, and touched the summit benchmark. A pair of pet Scotties bustled around near the old Tip Top House. A train was unloading. We made our way inside the summit building ahead of the freshly disembarked throng, seeking coffee.

We emerged refreshed and headed downward toward Tuckerman Ravine. Though humidity softened the long views, the day was warm and pleasant. As on all such summer days, the Tuckerman Ravine Trail was crowded with hikers. It is the shortest trail up Washington and is therefore heavily used. Leaving the last of the stairways and parking lots, we were in a loose line of people, picking their way downward through the jumbled rocks of the summit cone. We passed families with tots in sneakers and were passed, in turn, by clusters of chattering teenagers.

The trail drops directly down from the summit to the lip of Tuckerman Ravine, roughly approximating the route Thoreau followed through the fog with his compass. The crowds thinned out as we dropped over the edge of the ravine. Suddenly, our foursome was alone, stepping carefully along the cliffside path, which zigzagged down the steep sides of the ravine into which we were descending. Tuckerman Ravine is an immense half-bowl, carved by a prehistoric glacier out of gray bedrock. In the winter, it fills with snow and becomes a popular backcountry skiing destination.

There was no snow in evidence on the July day we descended deeper and deeper into the ravine. Water seeped and drizzled off the overhanging ledges, then coalesced into larger streams that bounded down the headwall in a series of misty waterfalls. The smaller seeps made moist little grottoes amidst the rocks where ferns, sedges, and wildflowers grew. Assemblages of of alpine sandwort and three-toothed cinquefoil, harebells, and mountain avens decorated the rock walls beside our path.

In one of the little grottoes, I found a delicate grouping of tall leafy white orchis—a tiny mountain orchid—and farther down there was a nice stand of pale painted cup, pastel pinks and creams against the gray bedrock. Once again, I felt close to Thoreau. He might well have seen similar wildflowers—though in the cooler climate of July 1858, he had slipped on the remnants of the winter snowfields.

The yellow blossoms of arnica—the plant Thoreau had used to help reduce the swelling in his sprained ankle—were fading now, but the plant was still easily recognizable. Creeping snowberry (which Thoreau brewed up for "chiogenes tea") was evident. The newly set fruits of the little clumps of bunchberry were still small, not yet the bright red-orange they would be in a couple of weeks, and the beadlike fruit of the abundant clintonia were just beginning to turn blue. I dropped back to enjoy the early-summer wildflowers and escape the need for conversation.

We picked our way down the Little Headwall—the trail a series of stone staircases—walked across the board bridges that skirt the north side of Hermit Lake, and rested at the ranger station just beyond. Then we headed down the wide trail to Pinkham Notch, two miles below, with the evening song of the winter wren in our ears.

Just east of the little crossroads of Jefferson, New Hampshire, with its stores and gas stations, U.S. Route 2 rises to a height of land. There, the striking panorama of the White Mountains that Thoreau saw on July 13, 1858, can be seen today. The great stone-capped sweep of the

Presidential Range marches southward from Mount Madison in the north to beyond Mount Washington. Mounts Garfield, Lafayette, and others are also visible, with the peaked, tentlike form of Cherry Mountain closer at hand. It is very similar to the view that Thoreau saw after a rainstorm and described as "the grandest mountain view I ever got."

There are differences, of course. Though it is a two-lane highway, Route 2 is one of the major east-west corridors across northern New England and is seldom deserted. Like most of New England, the land is more forested today than it was in the 19th century. One of the reasons you can see the view at all is because of a more contemporary recreational amenity—the golf course in the foreground. And even from this distance, the best way to identify Mount Washington is to look for the complex of broadcast towers on its summit.

The towers are not exactly picturesque. But they are part of an ongoing historical continuum involving the mountain, the people living in the valleys around it, and Thoreau himself. In his two climbs up Mount Washington, he saw the mountain change from a wilderness peak to a tourist attraction. It had been almost completely wild in 1839, but by 1858 had acquired bridle paths, the beginnings of a carriage road, and two summit hotels. Mountains had become Romantically popular, and the first influx of the tourist industry had arrived on Mount Washington.

More was soon to come. More buildings, a stone "observation tower," and a smoking, puffing, tootling (and, technically, quite amazing) cog railroad. And, of course, more people. After the Civil War, the summit of Mount Washington became one of New England's premier tourist destinations. It was called, without irony, the "city in the clouds."

Perhaps fortunately for his own peace of mind, Thoreau missed most of it. He died in 1862. His 1858 trip was his last visit to the mountain.

A disastrous fire in 1908 destroyed all of the 19th-century summit buildings except the Tip Top House (today a museum) and ended one era of tourism on the mountaintop. But a second soon began. The sprawling, concrete bunkerlike Sherman Adams Summit Building, the multiple communication towers, and the tiered parking lots on the mountain today are the culmination of that second round of development.

There is a certain tacky allure to the summit scene—the huffing, belching old train arriving in a cloud of smoke, the crowded bustle of the loading platform, and the great concrete restaurant/gift shop in the sky, the mixed aromas of damp hikers and stale coffee. Add to all that the fact that you're on a wild mountaintop surrounded by a striking array of bare, stony peaks, and the heady inconsistency of the mix can be entertaining. A busy state fair or a good, packed Chinatown market offers the same kind of crowd-induced rush.

And so you could argue that democracy is being served atop Mount Washington—that because of the road and the railway and the summit station more people can visit and enjoy the highest peak in New England. The young and fit (or the old and fit) who can clamber up a tough trail shouldn't be the only ones to experience the alpine beauty of the high Presidentials. Perhaps the environmental movement is better served in the long run by bringing the masses to the world above treeline and educating them. Perhaps the summit buildings help us avoid a shallow elitism.

Perhaps.

But more likely, the real god being served atop Mount Washington is not Democracy, but Mammon. The railway and the carriage road were begun as commercial enterprises and exist as commercial enterprises today. The state of New Hampshire, having invested several million dollars in the summit building and other accommodations, needs to recoup its investment. The fruition of the commercial society Thoreau so vigorously opposed 150 years ago now flourishes atop Mount Washington, visible for miles around.

In fact, no one today sees the pristine summit of Mount Washington. It is almost completely masked. In its place (literally) we have a paved state park, bristling with towers and buildings. If you want to find the mountain, don't go there. And in fact, many who love the White Mountains do not.

Thoreau grumbled about the two mountaintop hotel buildings of 1858 and felt that mountaintops should be considered sacred places. "I think that the top of Mt. Washington should not be private property," he wrote in his journal on January 3, 1861. "It should be left unappropriated, for modesty and reverence's sake, or if only to suggest that earth has higher uses than we put her to."

This thought drove Thoreau to an extended rant, in which he declared: "Thank God, men cannot as yet fly, and lay waste the sky as well as the earth!" The 21st century has added its own ironic footnote to that comment, since we are now busily doing both.

Thoreau's position—that mountaintops should belong to no one and be left alone—is clear, moral, and uncompromising. It was a very unusual stand for mid-19th-century America, much more unusual in Thoreau's day than in our own. His opposition to the commercial exploitation of nature is consistent and relentless.

The easy, slam-dunk position would be to endorse him. He is right, after all. But today that is an exercise in futile moralizing: enjoyable, satisfying, but ultimately quixotic—tilting at broadcast towers. Unfortunately, the towers and buildings atop New England, the traffic and the commerce, are likely to be permanent. They will be there longer than we are here.

Mount Washington, like most of the rest of New England, is a complex landscape of wilderness, commerce, and accommodation. It is both wild and not wild, both protected and exploited. It is the emblem of the compromised New England landscape we have created since Henry David Thoreau walked through it in the mid-1800s.

The wonder is that he saw it coming so early on.

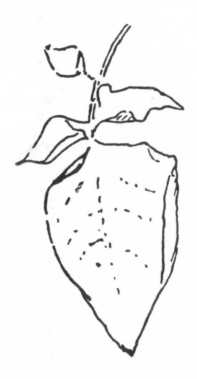

A leaf of the nightshade, sketch from Thoreau's journal, September 30, 1858

We are made to love the river and the meadow, as the wind to ripple the water."

—Journal, February 14, 1851

9

Conclusion: What's Left

The river talks quietly as the springtime dusk deepens. Shadows silently emerge from under each tree and fern; they rise out of the earth and fill the surrounding forest. Finally the sky darkens. My campfire crackles. I sit, watching it, and take a sip of bourbon. (Care for a taste, Henry? No? Fine. But please, stop scowling.)

I am indulging in a night out—literally. Sometimes after a long Vermont winter, I begin to feel confined by my life and most particularly by the walls of my house. I experience an almost physical need to make myself a camp in the woods, watch a fire burn down to ashes, and let a brook or river talk me to sleep.

I am fortunate to have a place to pursue this vice: the family farm, now owned by my sister, has about seventy acres of woodland that climb the hills alongside the Dog River. My campsite is barely a half-mile from the house and a paved road, but it is private enough. I can scorch a simple meal alongside the river and curl into my down sleeping bag without human interruption, except for my own thoughts—which lately almost always include Henry.

Tonight he pesters me about wildness. And wilderness. What has New England done to its wild lands? Are there any left? Do people care about them now? I have followed him for several years now, seeking out those places. What do I have to report?

First, let us define our terms. Thoreau went on at some length about wildness and wilderness; I know that he tried to use those terms precisely in his writing, and so have I. But neither of us has really bothered to define them properly. Therefore, I will make an attempt at clarification—the hobgoblin, I know, of lesser minds than Henry David's.

Roughly speaking—the only way one can speak about vague concepts—"wilderness" refers to a specific kind of place, usually an actual physical place that you can find on a map and visit: the Maine woods, the Pemigewasset Wilderness in the White Mountains, Katahdin, the Atlantic Ocean. "Wildness" is, in one sense, the quality you find in such places. But wildness—"the wild"—for Thoreau, meant a great deal more than just a quality, because it was more to him than an abstract concept. For Thoreau, wildness was immediate, present everywhere. It was nothing less than a driving force animating the universe, "the force that through the green fuse drives the flower," as Dylan Thomas once put it.

This is how Thoreau put it:

". . . in Wildness is the preservation of the World. Every tree sends its fibres forth in search of the Wild. The cities import it at any price. Men plow and sail for it. . . . I believe in the forest, and in the meadow, and in the night in which the corn grows."

In other words, he believed in the presence of wildness in both forest and meadow, and he believed in the mystery of this life: what makes the corn grow in the night? Wildness. Although he didn't identify it as such, Thoreau's allegiance was to what the Chinese called the Tao, the mysterious animating principle that Lao Tzu and other ancient philosophers believed empowers and drives all nature, including human nature. It is universal, as present in the oaks and maples shading Concord's streets as in the pine and fir forests of northern Maine. Thoreau's contemporary Walt Whitman was contemplating the same primordial force when he wrote, "I believe a leaf of grass is no less than the journey-work of the stars." Whether you call it wildness or Mother Nature or the Tao it exists everywhere.

And yet Thoreau obviously felt that wildness could been seen and appreciated better in some places than others. He preferred to find it out of town:

"Hope and the future for me are not in lawns and cultivated fields, not in towns and cities, but in the impervious and quaking swamps," he wrote. "I derive more of my subsistence from the swamps which surround my native town than from the cultivated gardens in the village."

He could sense wildness on the shores of Walden Pond and in the surrounding swamps and bogs and forests, even though those places were not unspoiled wilderness; they were part and parcel of the largely tamed countryside around Concord.

When he wanted more wildness, he sought it out by plunging into a wilderness. Going to wild places made him joyful and lighthearted and so he did it as often as he could, the less civilized, the better.

Although this place beside the Dog River is not a wilderness, I find him here also, at my humble forest campsite. And since wildness is here, so is Henry David Thoreau.

⚊ ⚊ ⚊

In following Thoreau around New England, I have gotten to know both him and the region better. Both, I have found, are considerably more than I at first assumed them to be.

New England today is clearly, manifestly, not the New England that Henry David Thoreau inhabited in the mid-1800s. Time and technology have transformed our society, and we—busy, educated, post-industrial, well-trained consumers that we are—have transformed this place in which we live.

Though nostalgia for the past and a cultivated affection for steam locomotives, covered bridges, and a small-scale pastoral world can make us wish otherwise, New England today differs radically from that earlier New England. It is a different place, with more prosperity and, perhaps, less soul—though Henry was pretty emphatic about the lack of soul in the New England of 1845.

Things are different now. Drive Interstate 95 (Route 128) around Boston any day of the week if you doubt it.

And yet, the glowing coals of my campfire assure me that you can still find wildness in staid and settled New England, and, to a somewhat more complicated degree, wilderness as well. There's actually a considerable amount of wilderness still left in the region, especially northern New England. But in almost every instance it exists provisionally, isolated pieces of a vanishing ecological frontier that our burgeoning society has pressed into enclaves, surrounded by roads and suburbs, and then "protected." There are probably a dozen definitions of wilderness, involving roadless areas, undisturbed old-growth forest, water quality, and so on. For me, defining wilderness is vaguer and simpler: I know it when I see it. Or when I'm in it.

One of my standards is that wilderness can kill you. Ironically one of our deadliest wild places is also one of the most easily accessible: the Presidential Range of the White Mountains. Though Mount Washington and the surrounding peaks of the Presidential Range are laced with trails and surrounded by roads, their bare upper slopes and unpredictable weather make them dangerous, year-round. Many have died of exposure there, even in summer.

One recent May, on the edge of that particular wilderness, I was quite sure I didn't need to go any farther into it. A friend and I were standing on granular, late-spring snowpack in Tuckerman Ravine on the east side of Mount Washington. We had hiked in on a May morning that was warm and mostly sunny—in the valley. But by the time we had climbed the two miles from Pinkham Notch up and into the bowl of the ravine, the sky directly above us was black and howling. The benign-looking beret of clouds Mount Washington had been wearing as we drove to its base was, in fact, a summit storm that sounded up close like a mini-cyclone. Where we stood in the ravine, the air was calm. A slightly clammy mist had settled into the snow-filled bowl. But on the heights above, the wind was roaring. It sounded alive—like an immense, unbelievably violent beast—powerful enough to quickly sap our strength and snuff out our insignificant lives.

"I don't think we should go up there," I said, exercising my talent for understatement.

"Right. No way," my friend quickly agreed, looking behind him to make sure the trail out was still there. A handful of snowboarders were skimming down carefully through the mist. They weren't climbing above the rim of the ravine either.

We beat a hasty retreat back to Pinkham Notch, where partly sunny skies and mild spring breezes still prevailed. It was hard to believe that the raging wilderness into which we had peered and from which we had retreated was the same place that on a mild summer day would see lines of tourists, clad in shorts and T-shirts, picking their way slowly uphill toward the summit buildings and parking lots. But it was.

<hr />

New England's history is long and complex, and our wild places share in that complexity. Every place that Thoreau treasured was caught in the flux of change when he knew it and has been altered since.

Consider, for example, Walden Pond, the epicenter of Thoreau's life and world. It has endured a century-long cycle of damage and restoration. No wilderness in Thoreau's time, it is not wilderness in ours. But at least some of its wild nature has survived the 150 years of change it has endured.

Even while Thoreau lived at the pond, the woods around it were being logged. The process continued after he left his cabin there, and he complained about it in Walden:

"Since I left those shores the woodchoppers have still further laid them waste, and now for many a year there will be no more rambling through the aisles of the wood. . . . My muse may be excused if she is silent henceforth," he wrote. "How can you expect the birds to sing when their groves are cut down?"

Though Walden Pond remained a pretty spot, its ecology and that of the surrounding woods went into a long, gradual decline. Logging, the demand for firewood, and forest fires depleted the forest, and many who went there commented on the damage. The impression that Walden Pond was a sylvan retreat, created in no small part by *Walden*, was rudely shattered for people who actually visited it. A guidebook of the late 19th century noted that the the pond and woods around "have been much changed by forest fires and the wood cutter."

W. Barksdale Maynard's wonderful book *Walden Pond: A History* carefully records the pond's decline, noting that sections of the nearby woods were clear-cut and their ecological variety diminished, both during Thoreau's stay there and afterward. He quotes botanist Richard J. Eaton, who wrote in the 1950s that repeated forest fires around the pond had decimated several species of plants known to Thoreau.

In the 1870s and 1880s an amusement park and picnic grounds, "Lake Walden," flourished at the west end of the pond (next to the railroad known to Thoreau thirty years earlier—which provided transportation to and from Boston). Summer crowds there often numbered in the thousands.

Later, a public beach served by public roads was established at the pond's east end; by the 1930s, it had become popular enough to be a source of concern. Thoreau's followers—themselves a growing tribe by then—recognized the beach early on as a threat to the contemplative serenity that Thoreau had celebrated.

The problem (as Concord resident Jayne Gordon, then director of the Thoreau Society, pointed out to me when we walked the nearby woods) was that the pond had long been used for swimming and fishing by local people—including Thoreau and Emerson. And so when the Emersons conveyed the pond to the county, the Deed of Gift specifically protected those activities—a decision later generations of Emersons might have come to regret. Mass transportation, first the railroad, then automobiles, brought exponentially greater numbers of visitors, and the problems of overuse grew.

Less than a century after Thoreau lived there, the east end of the pond had acquired a busy paved highway, concrete walks, bathhouses, gas stations, a couple of hot dog stands, and, just across the road and up from the pond, the Concord Town Dump. The writer E.B. White visited in 1939, and found the pond littered and depressing. He wrote a scathingly ironic essay in which he said to Henry:

"I knew I must be nearing your woodland retreat when the Golden Pheasant lunchroom came into view—Sealtest ice cream, toasted sandwiches, hot frankfurters, waffles, tonics, and lunches. . . . Beyond the Pheasant was a place called Walden Breezes."

The Breezes, directly opposite the public beach, offered, along with hot dogs, shakes, and fried clams, an amenity advertised on a sign since lost to posterity: "Bathing Suits for Rent."

The east end of the pond thus became devoted to commerce, while those interested in solitude, contemplation, or literature (a decidedly smaller crowd) found solace in the west end, which is the location of Thoreau's Cove, the memorial cairn, and cabin site.

The growing indignation of Thoreau's followers broke into open hostility in June of 1957 when the Middlesex County Commissioners deployed bulldozers to construct a new beach on the pond's northeast shore. Swimmers called the spot Red Cross Beach, but it was revered as "the fireside" by Thoreauvians. (The phrase was from *Walden*; the northeast shore was the spot where Thoreau went to warm himself on sunny late-fall days.)

Trees were slashed down and the bulldozers began pushing sand and soil out into the pond. For Thoreau's followers, it was the last straw. They rallied their supporters, hired lawyers, and denounced the expansion in local and national news media. Ultimately, they won. A court injunction stopped the beach expansion, and the ravaged bank was gradually restored. A single admirer of Thoreau's, Mary Sherwood, did much of the work, planting many young trees. Thoreau Society members today refer to the wooded bank as "Sherwood's Forest."

After that episode it was clear that events were running out of control. Thoreau lovers realized they would have to fight to save Walden Pond. The nationally known writer and naturalist Edwin Way Teale, addressing the Thoreau Society in 1958, declared that forces implicit in mainstream American society would destroy both Walden Pond and Thoreau's ideals, unless controlled:

"You and I want to enjoy Walden Pond. And what happens? We find ourselves fighting for a pond to enjoy!" he said.

The Thoreau Society's outrage and the nascent environmental movement of the 1970s, combined with the county's mismanagement, resulted in the pond being turned over to the state Natural Resources Department. A new management plan with more emphasis on preservation was drafted. It aimed at limiting visitors to a thousand per day. The ugliest aspects of the east-end beach (two small cinderblock bathhouses and a concrete esplanade) were removed and the other swimming facilities were spruced up. Most important of all, parking regulations were enforced: a new parking lot controlled access to the pond and limited cars to three hundred per day.

Greater threats arose and were beaten back. It took a determined battle of more than ten years plus several million dollars to stop developments—condominiums in one spot and a huge office complex in another—that would have filled the woods around Walden Pond with buildings and deeply compromised the pond itself. But the fight was waged and won. Today conserved forests surround most of the pond and many of the nearby places that Thoreau treasured are unspoiled. (See Chapter Two, "A Walk in the Concord Woods.")

The wire "concentration-camp" fences along the pondside path that shock many on their first visit were installed to protect Walden's steep banks from erosion. They serve an important purpose: if the thin, fragile topsoil of the banks is broken by a careless climber, rains drive dirt and sand into the pond. Once you are familiar with the pond's trails, it is easy to avoid the fences.

And so Walden Pond today is a mix of the sacred and the profane. It was not a wild place when Thoreau lived beside the pond and it is not a wild place today. A balance has been struck between society's relentless demand for recreation, *lebensraum*, fun—and the deep human need that Thoreau expressed for nature's beauty, solitude, and quiet contemplation. You can find both at Walden.

In its complexity the pond is emblematic of almost every other place that Thoreau loved. They are all, to some degree, environmentally complicated. New England's history is long and complex, and its wild places share in that complexity. They all exist in tenuous balance, each place threatened in some way, each place a compromise.

- Cape Cod's great outer arm, which Thoreau returned to several times for its raw beauty, is less raw today, and is no longer an environmental disaster. It is still beautiful, still essentially untamed because of its proximity to the wild Atlantic Ocean. But it is now part of Vacationland (as Thoreau himself had predicted). The Cape is now linked to the ever-churning engine of America's recreation economy. Were it not for the protection of the Outer Cape offered by the Cape Cod National Seashore, even the Great Beach would long ago have been developed.
- The grandeur of the Presidential Range is protected by the White Mountain National Forest, but the summit of Mount Washington, its highest peak, is drastically overdeveloped. A road (begun as a carriage road in Thoreau's time) and a 19th-century cog railway now bring tourists to its summit by the hundreds, where they are greeted by a stupendous view—plus communications towers, parking lots, and a large concrete summit building.
- Mount Monadnock, the mountain that Thoreau returned to most often, is located in a New Hampshire State Park, which offers it some protection from the many thousands of hikers who climb it. It is a dramatic and interesting mountain, close to Boston and the sprawling Northeastern megalopolis. As a result, Monadnock is climbed relentlessly by hordes of nature lovers who crowd its summit on sunny days. It is vigorously popular, undeniably overused. Other Massachusetts

peaks admired by Thoreau are developed to a greater or lesser degree, and are much visited. Wachusett and Greylock have paved summit roads. Yet even there, you can find free-running brooks and enclaves of wildness on their flanks.

• The forests of northern Maine that drew Thoreau like a magnet are still New England's largest wild area. Much of it is uninhabited, certifiably wilderness. Yet the great forests have been logged repeatedly and now, because of shifting ownership patterns, face the strong possibility of widespread recreational development.

• Katahdin, the "greatest mountain" that fascinated Thoreau throughout his life, has been firmly protected thanks to the heroic lifelong campaign of former Maine governor Percival Baxter. It may be the exception, the one place Thoreau's vision of true wildness-in-wilderness lives on. Yet even there, the pressure for more access is intense. In summer, cars line up before dawn at the entry gate to Baxter State Park and Katahdin's summit is seldom deserted. Were it not for the personal fortune of Governor Baxter and his determination that the park remain a wilderness, it too would likely be compromised.

Nevertheless, more of Thoreau's New England remains than you might expect. The amazing regenerative power of our major ecosystem, the Northern Forest, has healed many of the wounds inflicted on the region. The Concord forests that Thoreau walked in are in better shape now than they have been for a century. Cape Cod's once-devastated landscape has recovered so thoroughly that open heathlands, which once dominated the Outer Cape, have become an increasingly rare environmental community and are protected in some spots. The Cape's shifting sands have been stabilized by a restored forest of pitch pine and scrub oak. The timber cutting and agricultural clearing that had deforested much of New England has ended. Now farming in the region is endangered and the forests have returned to cover eighty percent of the land and more. You could argue that the region's overall ecology is better off today than it was 150 years ago.

The problem is that we are busily inflicting other, subtler wounds on the wild landscapes and areas of true wilderness that remain. It is now more profitable to develop land in most of the region than it is to farm or log it—and so the working landscape that once typified the region is now being turned into subdivisions, shopping centers, and high-tech industrial parks. Because of the incredible amount of wealth our economic system has created—the same system Thoreau decried, early on—many of the new developments, especially in rural northern New England, are vacation homes occupied only a small part of the year. And thanks to new construction technologies and all that available money, houses can now be built in locations that were inaccessible or marginal before: ridgetops, filled-in wetlands, steep and rocky mountainsides.

Consequently, wherever open land is not protected in some fashion—by conservation easement, national forest, state park, or whatever—it is likely to be developed. The message regarding New England's open lands is quite clear: protect them or lose them.

For example, consider Concord and nearby Lexington.

Henry Thoreau's hometown of Concord has set aside a large portion of its total area as conserved lands. Consequently, many of the places Thoreau treasured—Heywood's Meadow, the Andromeda Ponds, Brister's Hill and others—are still unspoiled and intact. (However, Fair Haven Cliffs, with the fine views Thoreau described, is inaccessible because of private residential development.) Concord village, buffered from the suburban outwash of Boston by Minuteman National Historical Park, is still recognizably Concord—a tidy Massachusetts village set at the confluence of the Sudbury and Assabet rivers. Its downtown is busy and vital. It still feels like a place—like itself, the town Henry Thoreau lived in.

But due east, just the other side of the pretty fields and forests of the national historical park, things change. In Lexington, you're back in an urban free-fire zone: relentless traffic, suburban sprawl, strip development, and not much evidence of conserved open space until, driving westward, you enter the national historical park again. Lexington is not an especially bad example of an urban fringe; Concord is not Arcadia. But the contrast between the two towns is striking; in one you're in the heart of the beast—a suburban piece of the great sprawling metropolis of Northeastern America. In the other, you're back in New England. Land conservation works.

— — —

In searching for Thoreau's New England, I found Thoreau. Tracking him up mountains and along rivers and beaches brought me face to face with him in a way I hadn't experienced before.

Walking with him as a companion beside the crashing Atlantic surf helped me appreciate—assimilate, really—the buoyant good humor of his writing in *Cape Cod*. Finding mountain flowers blooming in the White Mountains precisely where he described them blooming gave me a hint of his achievement as a botanist. Following his footsteps in Maine gave me some feeling for the great scope of his travels there. On Katahdin, fighting my way down the mountain and out of a thunderstorm, I felt the raw power of nature that impressed him.

And in some hard-to-define way, my travels and reading helped me encounter his quirky, obdurate personality. My understanding of this brilliant, cantankerous man has deepened—as have my admiration and affection for him. In going where he went, seeing what he saw, and feeling what I imagined he may have felt, I have come to know and like him better.

There's no question that he could be a hard person to like, both in his own time and ours. He took a certain enjoyment in being confrontational, even outrageous. His opposition to conventional Christianity was partially a stance, consciously taken, to shock conventional churchgoers. Thoreau also had a wry, perverse sense of humor that often poked fun—sometimes with sharp-edged accuracy—at its subjects. His portrait of an old Cape Cod woman made his lecture audiences laugh, but angered Cape Codders. There are quips and jokes about his companions throughout his writings. And he was relentless, especially in the pages of *Walden*, in his criticism of his Concord neighbors.

None of which sat well with his targets. Most of the people of Concord apparently did not think well of the over-educated, under-employed, iconoclastic loafer who (in their view) kept poking at them. Concord's resentment lasted for years. Thoreau biographer Walter Harding used to tell the story of the sweet old Concord woman who regularly visited Sleepy Hollow Cemetery to bedeck the graves on Author's Ridge with flowers: first Emerson's imposing stone, then each of the Alcotts, then Hawthorne's. Then she would spin around to face Thoreau's grave, just across the path, and snap: "And none for you, you dirty little atheist!"

Actually, with a mind as vigorous and protean as Thoreau's, it is hard to make generalizations that stick. He could be witty, elegant, even profound. He was sometimes petty, sometimes digressive, very seldom conventionally graceful. Often, he could be infuriatingly stubborn, even when he knew he was wrong—perhaps most of all when he knew he was wrong.

And yet by remaining true to his vision and to himself, he has become a part of our contemporary world and contemporary thought. *Walden* has been translated into a dozen foreign languages. His essay "Civil Disobedience" has informed protest movements around the globe, inspiring both Gandhi and Martin Luther King. The modern environmental movement looks to Thoreau as one of its spiritual ancestors. His thinking has become part of our assumptions about the natural world, and he has provided inspiration for many of our great environmental writers and thinkers: John Muir, Aldo Leopold, Henry Beston, Edward Abbey, Berndt Heinrich, Bill McKibben, and others.

"The man who burned the forest," scorned by Concord in his own day, has become in our own time a part of our consciousness and our heritage as Americans.

Why? Why is Henry David Thoreau, who was regarded as—at best—a minor disciple of Emerson while alive, now so vitally important to our contemporary experience? Why is he the only Transcendentalist we still read willingly?

One reason is simply that he was a terrific writer. His prose is entertaining: vigorous, imaginative, full of wit and energy. To be honest, his prose could and did wander off into boring digressions and minutiae. *A Week on the Concord and Merrimack Rivers* is hard to plow through for just that reason. And yet even that book has its moments.

At its best, Thoreau's writing is magical. Consider the following passage from his journal: "To make a perfect winter day like this, you must have a clear, sparkling air, with a sheen from the snow, sufficient cold, little or no wind; and the warmth must come directly from the sun. It must not be a thawing warmth. The tension of nature must not be relaxed. The earth must be resonant if bare, and you hear the lisping tinkle of chickadees from time to time and the unrelenting steel-cold scream of a jay, unmelted, that never flows into a song, a sort of wintry trumpet, screaming cold; hard, tense, frozen music, like the winter sky itself; in the blue livery of winter's band. It is like a flourish of trumpets to the winter sky. There is no hint of incubation in the jay's scream. Like the creak of a cart-wheel. There is no cushion for sounds now. They tear our ears."

One learns to skim when Thoreau lurches into a long, tedious digression—about, say, the history of Evangelical preaching on Cape Cod (near the end of his chapter on Eastham, "The Plains of Nauset"). But even in such instances, he often seems aware of what he is doing. At the end of that particular long digression, which includes quotations from several old sermons and town histories, he notes playfully:

"There was no better way to make the reader realize how wide and peculiar that plain was, and how long it took to traverse it, than by inserting these extracts in the midst of my narrative."

More often his writing is beautiful and insightful. It can skim along the surface of his observations like a flung stone, then suddenly plunge to astonishing depths:

"As I come over the hill, I hear the wood thrush singing his evening lay. This is the only bird whose note affects me like music, affects the flow and tenor of my thought, my fancy and imagination. It lifts and exhilarates me. It is inspiring. It is a medicative draught to my soul. It is an elixir to my eyes and a fountain of youth to all my senses. It changes all hours to an eternal morning. It banishes all trivialness."

Henry Thoreau wasn't the first person to climb Katahdin, nor the first Yankee to symbolically withdraw from society and go live in a forest hut. But he captured those experiences in words more vivid and compelling than any written before—and most written after. Both *Cape Cod* and *The Maine Woods* still sell steadily.

The other reason Thoreau has lasted is that he stood for something—something that is important to us today. It is easy to forget now, with the principles of ecology, conservation, civil disobedience, and conscious alternatives to mainstream society well established, how unusual and courageous it was to stand for such things in mid-19th-century America and in staid old Concord, Massachusetts. But Thoreau saw the coming of the commercial age, and (conveniences and luxuries notwithstanding) the threat it posed to the places he cared about. He railed against the way it made willing slaves of those who bought into it. He saw, early on, how crass and superficial American life could become; he fought against those tendencies vigorously (and, one has to admit, inconsistently). He could not have forseen the coming world of mass communication, cellphones, supermarkets, super-sized meals and super-sized cars, the Internet and telemarketing. But he saw the seed of it all, sprouting, in the mindless labor of his Concord neighbors, the pillaging of the lands around Walden Pond and the forests of Maine, and our human fascination with new technologies (the railroad and telegraph in his day). He saw the unthinking allegiance to speed, commerce, and profit that was emerging in the 19th century and that dominates the 21st. And he saw—clearly and brilliantly—the threat that those emerging forces posed for both untrammeled nature, and the human spirit.

Those forces have not gone away. In fact, they have become more universal and perilous, even as they have made our lives easier. And so Thoreau has become ever more relevant to our current predicament. The late Edward Abbey, a writer and naturalist who was as obdurate and uppity as Henry Thoreau himself, puts it well:

"The deeper our United States sinks into industrialism, urbanism, militarism—with the rest of the world doing its best to emulate America—the more poignant, strong, and appealing becomes Thoreau's demand for the right of every woman, every child, every dog, every tree, every snail darter, every lousewort, every living thing, to live its own life in its own way at its own pace in its own square mile of home. . . ."

Thoreau had an American dream; it ran counter to the one that has prevailed. But he remained eloquent and courageous and honest in proclaiming it. And stubborn as a stone.

And so he sits like a granite boulder in the mainstream of our national consciousness. His principles, his firm determination to live by them—to live, as he put it, deliberately—are plunked right athwart the onrushing flow of our society, and force it into turbulence.

He didn't spare himself. He knew, and noted in his journal, that by surveying the woods around Walden Pond, he was participating in their partition and logging. But that self-knowledge didn't make him bend his principles or stop his protest. His vision remained strong. And confrontational:

"I wish to speak a word for Nature, for absolute freedom and wildness, as contrasted with a freedom and culture merely civil,—to regard man as an inhabitant, or a part and parcel of Nature, rather than a member of society," he said at the beginning of the lecture that became part of his essay "Walking."

"I wish to make an extreme statement, if so I may make an emphatic one, for there are enough champions of civilization: the minister and the school committee and every one of you will take care of that."

It is that hard clarity—and the consummate skill with which he expressed it—that still speaks today to those who will listen.

— — —

The embers of my campfire have burned low. They are settling down for the night, and so am I.

I heard a barred owl call a few minutes ago; now it is silent, probably hunting, its great, dark eyes searching through the forest for furtive movement. Fortunately, the blackflies are not out in force yet. Jack-in-the-pulpits are unfurling in the woods. False hellebore has sprouted its cabbage-like shoots alongside the river, which burbles softly as the night deepens.

The land has remembered spring. Here, and across New England, the sweet, wild ritual of emerging life has begun once more. The wild still lives in New England, still has the power to calm and heal us.

Perhaps that is our greatest intellectual legacy from Henry Thoreau —his belief that nature, "wildness," is not something exotic, apart from us, something that we must go someplace to visit. Because every untrammeled place is infused with—inseparable from—wildness, all of it is worthy and valuable, this hillside swatch of second-growth forest a half-mile from the highway, as well as the great forests of northern Maine; this small river as well as the Atlantic Ocean that pounds against the Outer Beach of Cape Cod.

We do not live alone, but in an interconnected web with every other being, human and otherwise. Nature is not separate from us; it is interwoven with every aspect of our world and of ourselves. And the more we look for that simple fact, the more we find it. And this, too, is part of our legacy from Henry. He was the first American writer to voice the idea that we humans have a deep-seated need to connect with nature, and that nature is therapeutic. Many writers have voiced it since, because of its obvious truth. It is a notion now deeply lodged in our national consciousness. Not only do we need wild nature—wild nature needs us back. We are the only ones who can protect it, after all. We need the wild lands of New England, and they need our care and commitment. We are interdependent.

Henry's ghost sees me dozing, and wanders off, following the river-bank downstream. Well, you were always one for night walks, I think to myself as I fall asleep to the whispering of the river.

In the morning the sky is bright, clear blue, and ten thousand birds are singing noisily, happily.

Henry David Thoreau

Chronology

July 12, 1817: Born in Concord, Massachusetts

August 30, 1837: Graduated from Harvard College.

May 1838: Travels from Boston to Portland, Maine, by boat. Visits several Maine towns unsuccessfully seeking employment as a teacher. At Old Town, he talks with an elderly Penobscot man who tells him about "one beautiful country" farther north.

August/September 1839: Trip on Concord and Merrimack rivers to White Mountains and summit of Agiocochook (Mount Washington) with brother, John.

July 1841: Hikes to Mount Wachusett with Richard Fuller.

July/August 1844: Hikes with poet Ellery Channing to Mount Monadnock, then walks west, alone, to summit of Mount Greylock (Saddleback) in western Massachusetts, then on to Catskills in New York before returning to Concord.

July 4, 1845: Moves into his hand-built cabin on Walden Pond.

August/September 1846: First trip to Maine woods. Goes by boat and rail to Bangor, then upriver by bateau; climbs to near summit of Katahdin. Returns by foot and bateau to Bangor, then by boat to Boston.

July 1847: Leaves Walden Pond, lives with Emerson's family in Concord.

October 1849: First trip to Cape Cod, with Ellery Channing. Travels by train to Cohasset and Sandwich, then by stagecoach to Eastham. Walks on the Cape's Outer Beach from Eastham to Provincetown, stays overnight with "Wellfleet Oysterman," visits Cape Cod (Highland) Light in Truro, returns by steamer to Boston.

July 1850: To Fire Island, New York, to search for Margaret Fuller's body and belongings after her death in a shipwreck. Description of a corpse on beach (not Fuller's) later used in *Cape Cod*.

September 1850: Traverses Vermont by rail and Lake Champlain by steamer on way to Canada. Few comments on Vermont. In Canada visits Montreal and Quebec.

September 1852: Climbs Mount Monadnock with Ellery Channing.

September 1853: Second trip to Maine; by stagecoach from Bangor to Greenville, then takes steamer the length of Moosehead Lake to Northeast Carry. With guide Joe Aitteon and George Thatcher descends West Branch of the Penobscot River to Chesuncook Lake and returns. Thatcher bags a moose on the way to Chesuncook. Camps with Penobscot Indians on return trip.

October 1854: Hikes Mount Wachusett with Harrison Blake and Thomas Cholmondeley.

July 1855: Second trip to Cape Cod; by steamer to Provincetown. Hikes with Channing to Cape Cod (Highland) Light and other spots in Truro. Returns to Boston via steamer.

September 1856: By train to Brattleboro and Bellows Falls, Vermont, where he climbs Chesterfield (Wantastiquet) and Fall Mountains. Visits Bronson Alcott in Walpole, New Hampshire.

June 1857: Last trip to Cape Cod; by train to Plymouth, then Sandwich, walks to Cape Cod Light and Provincetown. Returns to Boston via steamer.

July/August 1857: Third and last trip to Maine woods; by train to Portland, steamer to Bangor, stage to Greenville. He and Penobscot guide Joe Polis and Edward Hoar paddle the length of Moosehead Lake. Thoreau and Hoar climb Mount Kineo. The party proceeds down the West Branch to Chesuncook Lake, then on to Chamberlain Lake, Eagle Lake, and down Webster Stream to Grand Lake Matagamon and the East Branch of the Penobscot. Returns by train to Portland and by steamer to Boston.

June 1858: Climbs Mount Monadnock with Harrison Blake.

July 1858: By horse and wagon with Hoar to White Mountains. Climbs Mount Washington, sprains ankle in Tuckerman Ravine, where the party meets Harrison Blake and Theo Brown, as planned; through Gorham and Jefferson, New Hampshire, to Franconia Notch; climbs Mount Lafayette.

September 1858: Walking trip to Cape Ann, North Shore of Massachusetts: Salem, Marblehead, Beverly, Gloucester.

August 1860: Climbs Mount Monadnock with Channing.

May to July 1861: Travels to Minnesota in an unsuccessful attempt to regain his health.

May 6, 1862: Dies at family home in Concord, Massachusetts.

When You Go:

Tips on Tracking Thoreau

1. Walden Pond: The pond lies due south of Concord village. Massachusetts Route 2, the main east-west highway in the area, swings south of Concord. Follow it to its intersection with Route 126 and turn south to the pond, which will be almost immediately on your right (parking lots are on the left). To get there from the village, follow Walden Street to the Route 2–Route 126 intersection, where it becomes Route 126.

Unless you hike over from Concord, you'll have to park in the designated, closely supervised parking lots on Route 126 (Walden Street). In summer, these lots fill early with cars packed with swimmers, so plan to get there before 9AM, even earlier if possible. Or avoid the summer months. The pond is a beautiful place year-round. Trail maps are available at the parking lots or the Thoreau Society gift shop nearby. The fenced-in shoreline walk to Thoreau Cove and the cabin site can be avoided by walking along Ridge Path, which is marked and follows the forested ridge above the pond's eastern shore. In addition to the cabin site, visits to Ice Fort Cove and Emerson's Cliff (on the opposite shore from the cabin site) are worthwhile. A walk around the pond takes about an hour.

The Thoreau Society, founded in 1941, is the oldest and largest organization devoted to an American author and is dedicated to promoting Thoreau's life and works through education, outreach, and advocacy. The society's website, www.thoreausociety.org, provides links to events and publications, and to related initiatives and research, such as the

Walden Woods Project, the Thoreau Institute at Walden Woods, and the Friends of Walden Pond.

2. Walden Woods and Concord Village: Surrounding Walden Pond are miles of beautiful trails leading to places that were important to Thoreau, and remain unspoiled today. However, the trails are not well marked, so local inquiry is recommended. Ask at the Town Clerk's office for maps. A new path up Brister's Hill (on the northeast corner of the busy intersection between Route 126 and Route 2) is marked with inscribed quotations from Thoreau's writings. Concord is an attractive village with a strong sense of its history and many beautiful houses. It is still recognizable as the town Thoreau was born in, the village he once described as "the most estimable place in all the world." Efforts are underway to restore the house he was born in on Virginia Road. The Thoreau Farm Trust is engaged in a campaign to purchase and restore the homestead, which is badly deteriorated, but when restored will be a prime example of an 18th-century New England farmhouse. The building is on the National Register of Historic Places. For information contact the Thoreau Farm Trust at www.thoreaufarm.org. None of the other houses of the Thoreau family remains, but a granite historical marker with a brass plaque shows the site of the jailhouse where he spent a night in 1846 for refusing to pay his Massachusetts poll tax. Visits to the Emerson House, where Thoreau lived from time to time, and the Concord Museum, which has a room filled with Thoreau memorabilia, are also worthwhile. They are located near one another on Cambridge Turnpike, just off Lexington Road on the east end of town.

The most evocative site, however, is Author's Ridge in the beautifully landscaped Sleepy Hollow Cemetery, where Henry lies alongside other members of the Thoreau family. Nearby are the graves of his friends and contemporaries: Hawthorne, Emerson, Louisa May and the other Alcotts. His lifelong friend Edward Hoar's grave is just down the hill, in the shadow of the ridge. The cemetery is north of the village center on Bedford Street. Signs within its gates will direct you to Author's Ridge.

3. The Concord and Merrimack Rivers: The Concord River flows north and east out of Concord toward Lowell, where it joins the Merrimack. Great Meadows Wildlife Refuge is nearby. Now a wetland, it is a major bird sanctuary and an interesting spot to visit. Both the Concord and the Merrimack have become important recreational resources for fishermen, paddlers, and, where the water is clean, for swimmers. A good source of information on the Concord River and other rivers in the watershed is the Merrimack River Watershed Council, which every summer offers a series of guided river excursions and overnight trips. For a schedule of trips and other information: www.merrimack.org.

4. Mounts Monadnock, Wachusett, Wantastiquet, Greylock: The best guide for the many trails on Mount Monadnock is the *Southern New Hampshire Trail Guide* published by the Appalachian Mountain Club. The White Dot and White Cross Trails closely approximate Thoreau's routes up the mountain, but are often very crowded, especially on weekends. The Marlboro, Dublin, and Pumpelly Trails may more closely recreate his experience today. There are roads to the Wachusett and Greylock summits, which are developed. However, both mountains also offer interesting and worthwhile hikes. The Bellows Pipe Trail on the north flank of Greylock closely approximates Thoreau's route up that mountain. Each July Williams College sponsors a hike up the Bellows Pipe Trail commorating Thoreau's hike.

Bonus mountain: Wantastiquet (Chesterfield) Mountain. Thoreau didn't often venture into Vermont. He visited Brattleboro in 1856, and climbed Wantastiquet and Fall mountains in nearby New Hampshire. The trail up Mount Wantastiquet, which looms over downtown Brattleboro, Vermont, is easily found by turning north (left) at the New Hampshire end of the Route 119 bridge, which links downtown Brattleboro with New Hampshire. Or inquire locally.

5. Katahdin: The mountain that haunted Thoreau's dreams rises dramatically in north-central Maine, about two hours north of Bangor. Follow

Interstate 95 north from Bangor to Millinocket, then follow signs from downtown Millinocket to Baxter State Park and Katahdin. Access to the park is closely controlled. If you want to climb Katahdin, the best strategy—the only feasible one, really, unless you live nearby—is to reserve a campsite; you have to do this three months in advance. The mountain is big and can be dangerous. Do not attempt to climb it in bad weather. The trail that most closely approximates Thoreau's route (the route he *should* have taken!) is the Abol Trail. It ascends Abol Slide, which is steep and rocky. A visit to Little Abol Falls, along a half-mile trail that begins at Abol Campground, will give you a feeling for the sort of bushwhacking Thoreau unwisely decided upon. The surrounding area is very thickly forested. The top of the ridge that is probably the one Thoreau attained, between Baxter Peak and South Peak, is traversed by the Knife Edge Trail, which continues beyond South Peak across the narrow, exciting, and sometimes dangerous Knife Edge. Walking the portion of that trail between Baxter and South Peak, you can speculate on just where Thoreau's personal "cloud-factory" might have been.

6. The Maine Woods: This is a vast area, worthy of a lifetime of exploration. The route paddled by Thoreau, Joe Polis, and Edward Hoar in 1857, an interconnected series of lakes, ponds, and streams surrounding and extending beyond the Katahdin massif, still exists and is still followed by Thoreau enthusiasts today. The Northern Forest Canoe Trail encompasses much of that route and connects it with native canoe routes across northern Maine, New Hampshire, Vermont, and New York. Maps of the various sections of this 740-mile trail are available from their headquarters at P.O. Box 565, Waitsfield, Vermont, 05673, or www.northernforestcanoetrail.org. A map of the specific routes that Thoreau followed in his paddling forays and on Katahdin is available from www.thoreauwabanakitrail.org, as well as more information on the Thoreau-Wabanaki Trail, a designation of those routes by Maine Woods Forever, a conservation group.

Mount Kineo, which rises abruptly from Moosehead Lake, is a short, spectacular hike accessible by a regular motorboat ferry that crosses the lake from Rockwood. The Birches, north of Rockwood, and Chesuncook Lake House on the remote lake of the same name, are low-key, pleasant places to appreciate the deep beauty of this area. Greenville is a small tourist town at the foot of Moosehead Lake, and is a good base of operations for further explorations of the area. To get to Greenville from Skowhegan on U.S. Route 2 in west-central Maine, follow Route 150 north to Guilford, and then Routes 6 and 15 (combined, they follow the same road) north from there to Greenville. Rockwood is about a half-hour north of Greenville on Routes 6 and 15.

7. Cape Cod: Spring and fall are the best times to visit. Thoreau preferred fall. Avoid summer, when the roads and beaches are very crowded. Winter is an interesting time on the Cape, but most of the lodging places and restaurants will be closed after December, many of them earlier.

Cross onto the Cape at the Sagamore Bridge or Bourne Bridge and follow U.S. Route 6, a limited access road, thirty-five miles west to the Orleans rotary, gateway to the Outer Cape. Route 6 bears north, following the "arm" of the Outer Cape, and so should you. Stop first at the National Seashore visitor center on Route 6 in Eastham, for directions, introductory films, information on scheduled events, maps, etc. Any walk on the Great Beach will be rewarding. It fronts the Atlantic Ocean for thirty miles between Orleans and Provincetown and is accessible at many points (east) off Route 6. LeCount Hollow, Cahoon Hollow, and Newcomb Hollow in Wellfleet all have small parking lots that give access to the Great Beach. Ocean View Drive, which connects them, is a scenic road that follows the height of land for a few miles and offers nice views of the Atlantic. The view from the Marconi Station overlook off Route 6 in South Wellfleet is sensational, also from Highland Light in Truro. There is no beach access from either of these overlooks. Provincetown, a fishing village in Thoreau's day, is now an artists' town, still an interesting and unusual place. However, in summer it is jammed with throngs of tourists.

8. Mount Washington and the White Mountains: The Presidential Range, which includes Mount Washington, is located in the White Mountain National Forest in northern New Hampshire. Route 302 through Crawford Notch passes the site of Crawford's inn, where Henry and John Thoreau stayed in 1839. The old inn is long gone, but there is a modern hostel, run by the Appalachian Mountain Club, at the northern entrance to the notch, where some supplies and hiking information are available. Route 16 through Pinkham Notch gives access to trails up the east side of the mountain and the Mount Washington Auto Road, which was being built as a carriage road when Thoreau hiked up it in 1858. The AMC's headquarters in the White Mountains is here, and snacks, supplies and hostel-style lodging are offered as well (www.outdoors.org).

As indicated earlier, the development on the summit of Mount Washington is a mixed blessing. The Mount Washington Auto Road offers motorized access to the top of the mountain, but hiking up one of the many trails is a better way to understand Thoreau's experience on this immense mountain. The Tuckerman Ravine Trail is the shortest and most direct way to the summit, and can be crowded on good days. Do not attempt to ascend the mountain in bad weather. Many people have died above treeline, even in summer, because of poor judgment. The Huntington Ravine Trail, described in Chapter Eight, is dangerous and should be avoided by the casual hiker. There are many other places on the Presidential Range also worthy of exploration. The Appalachian Mountain Club's *White Mountain Guide* is the best guidebook, and the club's headquarters and visitor center in Pinkham Notch is a good place to obtain necessary information about weather conditions and routes. Many trails begin there.

Thoreau also climbed Mount Lafayette, in the Franconia Range. The Old Bridle Path, accessible from Franconia Notch, was his route and is now an enjoyable hiking trail. Access is from Interstate 93, which goes through Franconia Notch. There are many other points of interest in this spectacular mountain notch, some of which Thoreau commented upon.

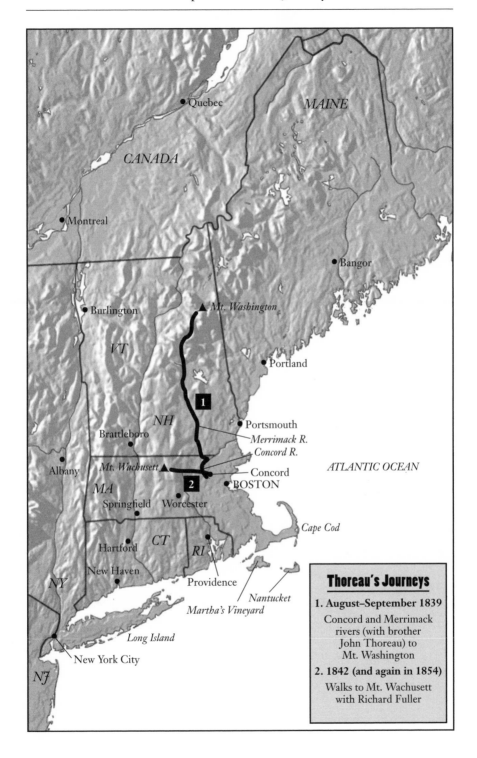

Quebec

MAINE

CANADA

Montreal

Bangor

Burlington

▲ Mt. Washington

VT

Portland

1

NH

Portsmouth

Brattleboro

Merrimack R.

Concord R.

Albany

Mt. Wachusett ▲

ATLANTIC OCEAN

MA

2

Concord

BOSTON

Springfield   Worcester

Cape Cod

Hartford

CT

RI

New Haven

NY

Providence

Nantucket

Martha's Vineyard

Long Island

NJ

New York City

Thoreau's Journeys

1. August–September 1839

Concord and Merrimack
rivers (with brother
John Thoreau) to
Mt. Washington

2. 1842 (and again in 1854)

Walks to Mt. Wachusett
with Richard Fuller

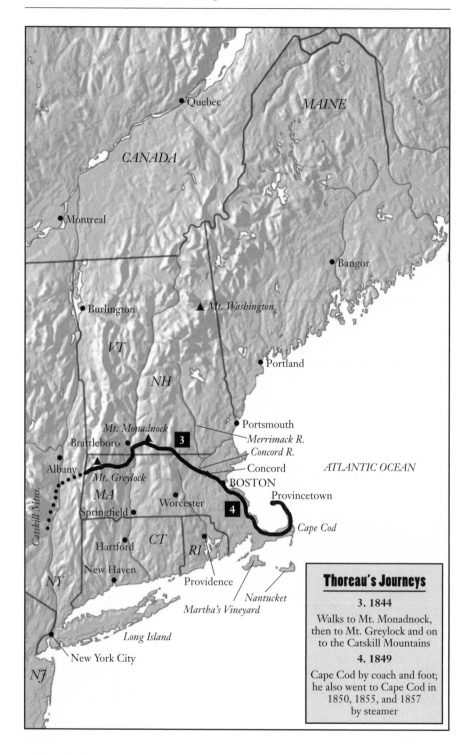

Quebec

MAINE

CANADA

Montreal

Bangor

Burlington

▲ Mt. Washington

VT

Portland

NH

Portsmouth

Mt. Monadnock   ▲   3   Merrimack R.

Brattleboro   Concord R.

Albany   ▲   Concord   ATLANTIC OCEAN

Mt. Greylock   BOSTON

MA

Worcester   Provincetown

Springfield   4

Cape Cod

Catskill Mtns.

CT

Hartford   RI

New Haven

NY   Providence

Nantucket

Martha's Vineyard

Long Island

New York City

NJ

Thoreau's Journeys

3. 1844

Walks to Mt. Monadnock,
then to Mt. Greylock and on
to the Catskill Mountains

4. 1849

Cape Cod by coach and foot;
he also went to Cape Cod in
1850, 1855, and 1857
by steamer

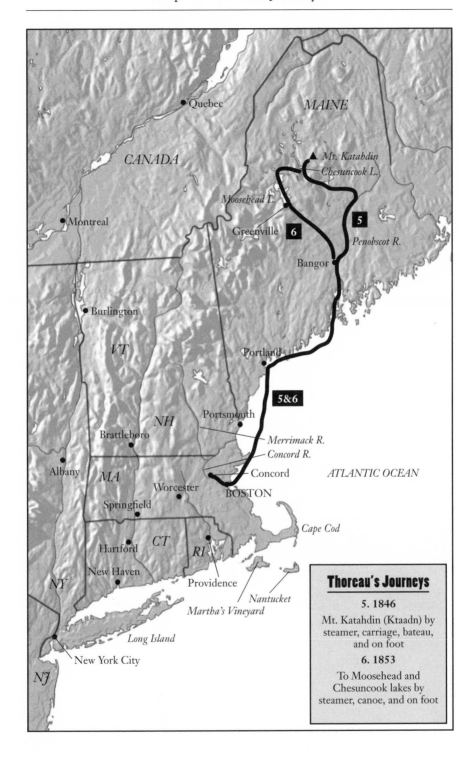

Quebec

MAINE

CANADA

▲ Mt. Katahdin

Chesuncook L.

Moosehead L.

Montreal

Greenville **6**

5

Penobscot R.

Bangor

Burlington

VT

Portland

Portsmouth

NH

5&6

Brattleboro

Merrimack R.

Concord R.

Albany

MA

Concord

ATLANTIC OCEAN

Worcester

BOSTON

Springfield

Cape Cod

Hartford

CT

RI

New Haven

NY

Providence

Nantucket

Martha's Vineyard

Long Island

New York City

NJ

Thoreau's Journeys

5. 1846

Mt. Katahdin (Ktaadn) by
steamer, carriage, bateau,
and on foot

6. 1853

To Moosehead and
Chesuncook lakes by
steamer, canoe, and on foot

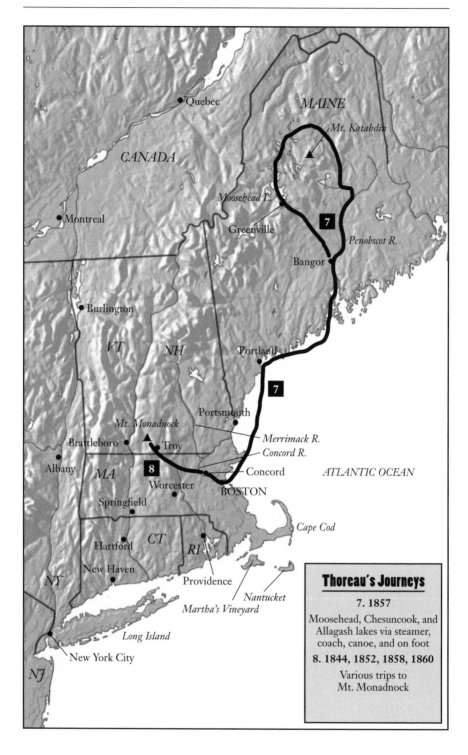

Quebec

MAINE

Mt. Katahdin

CANADA

Moosehead L.

Montreal

Greenville

7

Penobscot R.

Bangor

Burlington

VT   *NH*

Portland

Portsmouth

Mt. Monadnock

Brattleboro   Troy

7

Albany   *MA*

8

Worcester   Concord

Merrimack R.
Concord R.

BOSTON

ATLANTIC OCEAN

Springfield

Cape Cod

Hartford   *CT*   *RI*

New Haven

NY

Providence

Nantucket

Martha's Vineyard

Long Island

New York City

NJ

Thoreau's Journeys

7. 1857

Moosehead, Chesuncook, and
Allagash lakes via steamer,
coach, canoe, and on foot

8. 1844, 1852, 1858, 1860

Various trips to
Mt. Monadnock

Bibliography and Sources

By Henry David Thoreau

Quotations from the works of Henry David Thoreau in this book are from the editions listed below.

Walden, fully annotated edition, edited by Jeffrey S. Cramer; Yale University Press, 2004.

Walden, Princeton University Press, 2004.

The Maine Woods, Princeton University Press, 2004.

A Week on the Concord and Merrimack Rivers, Princeton University Press, 2004.

Cape Cod, Apollo Editions, Thomas Y. Crowell Co., New York, 1961.

The Essays of Henry David Thoreau, selected and edited by Lewis Hyde; North Point Press (Farrar, Straus and Giroux), 2002.

The Journal of Henry David Thoreau, edited by Bradford Torrey and Francis H. Allen, foreword by Walter Harding; Dover Publications, 1962.

The Portable Thoreau, edited by Carl Bode; Viking Press, 1964.

About Henry David Thoreau or his travels

A Thoreau Gazetteer, by Robert F. Stowell, edited by William Howarth; Princeton University Press, 1970.

Elevating Ourselves: Henry David Thoreau on Mountains, edited and with commentary by J. Parker Huber; Mariner Books, Houghton Mifflin Company, 1999.

Walking With Thoreau: A Literary Guide to the Mountains of New England, edited and with commentary by William Howarth; Beacon Press, 2001.

The Environmental Imagination: Thoreau, Nature Writing, and the Formation of American Culture, by Lawrence Buell; Harvard University Press, 1995.

The Days of Henry Thoreau: a Biography, by Walter Harding; Princeton University Press, 1982.

The New Thoreau Handbook, by Walter Harding and Michael Meyer; Gotham Library, New York University Press, 1980.

The Book of Concord: Thoreau's Life as a Writer, by William Howarth; Penguin Books, 1983.

The Cambridge Companion to Henry David Thoreau, edited by Joel Myerson; Cambridge University Press, 1995.

America's Bachelor Uncle: Thoreau and the American Polity, by Bob Pepperman Taylor, University Press of Kansas, 1996.

Henry Thoreau: A Life of the Mind, by Robert D. Richardson, Jr.; University of California Press, 1986.

Natural Life: Thoreau's Worldly Transcendentalism, by David M. Robinson; Cornell University Press, 2004.

Concord and Walden Pond

Thoreau's Country: Journey Through a Transformed Landscape, by David R. Foster; Harvard University Press, 1999.

Walden Pond: A History, by W. Barksdale Maynard; Oxford University Press, 2004.

Mount Monadnock and region

Where the Mountain Stands Alone: Stories of Place in the Monadnock Region, edited and with commentary by Howard Mansfield; University Press of New England, 2006.

Northern Maine and Katahdin

Chesuncook Memories by Lana Gagnon; Moosehead Communications Inc., June 1998.

The Wildest Country: A Guide to Thoreau's Maine, by J. Parker Huber; Appalachian Mountain Club, 1981.

Saving Maine: An Album of Conservation Success Stories, by Bill Silliker, Jr.; Downeast Books, 2002.

North to Katahdin, by Eric Pinder; Milkweed Editions, 2005.

Katahdin: An Historic Journey, by John W. Neff; Appalachian Mountain Club, 2006.

Cape Cod

The Outermost House, by Henry Beston; Viking Press, by arrangement with Holt, Rinehart & Winston, 1961.

A Place Apart: A Cape Cod Reader, edited by Robert Finch; W.W. Norton & Co., 1993.

Common Ground: A Naturalist's Cape Cod, by Robert Finch; David R. Godine, 1981.

Special Places on Cape Cod and the Islands, by Robert Finch; Commonwealth Editions, 2003.

In the Footsteps of Thoreau: 25 Historic & Nature Walks on Cape Cod, by Adam Gamble; On Cape Publications, 1997.

New England: history, natural history, literature

The Flowering of New England, 1815-1865, by Van Wyck Brooks; The Modern Library, Random House, 1936.

Literary New England: A History and Guide, by William Corbett; Faber & Faber, 1993.

Changes in the Land: Indians, Colonists, and the Ecology of New England, by William Cronon; Hill and Wang (Farrar, Straus and Giroux), 1983.

Inventing New England: Regional Tourism in the Nineteenth Century, by Dona Brown; Smithsonian Institution Press, 1995.

Forest & Crag: A History of Hiking, Trail Blazing, and Adventure in the Northeast Mountains, by Guy and Laura Waterman, Appalachian Mountain Club, 1989.

Trail guides

Maine Mountain Guide, eighth edition; Appalachian Mountain Club, Boston, 1999.

Southern New Hampshire Trail Guide, second edition, compiled and edited by Gene Daniell and Stephen D. Smith; Appalachian Mountain Club, 2005.

White Mountain Guide, twenty-sixth edition, compiled and edited by Gene Daniell and Jon Burroughs; Appalachian Mountain Club, 1998.

Massachusetts Hiking, by Michael Lanza, Avalon Publishing Group, Inc., 2005.

Notes and additional sources

p. vii: *Thoreau's Ecstatic Witness*, by Alan D. Hodder; Yale University Press, 2001.

p. 14: *Hayden Carruth: Selected Essays & Reviews*; Copper Canyon Press, 1996.

p. 56: Review of *A Week on the Concord and Merrimack Rivers in The Massachusetts Quarterly Review*, vol. III; Boston: Coolidge & Wiley, 1850.

p. 77: "Abbott Thayer in the Spell of Monadnock," by Richard Meryman, in *Where the Mountain Stands Alone: Stories of Place in the Monadnock Region.*

Society for the Protection of New Hampshire Forests newsletter, *Forest Notes*, summer 2006.

p. 90: From "Tintern Abbey," by William Wordsworth, 1798.

p. 96: Letter to Harrison Blake, November 16, 1857, quoted in *The Wildest Country.*

Thoreau's last words quoted in *The Days of Henry Thoreau.*

p. 112: Percival Baxter quoted in *Katahdin: An Historic Journey.*

p. 116: Information about logging and dams from "The Last Log Drive," by Marc Johnson, *Northern Woodlands Magazine*, autumn 2006.

p. 141: Thoreau's comment about Ellen Sewall quoted in *The Days of Henry Thoreau.*

p. 159: Information about Thoreau and Hoar's plant search from *The Days of Henry Thoreau.*

p. 161: *New York Tribune* article of July 17, 1858, quoted in *The Days of Henry Thoreau.*

p. 172: "The Force That through the Green Fuse Drives the Flower," by Dylan Thomas, 1933.

From *Leaves of Grass*, by Walt Whitman, 1855.

p. 177: "Walden," in *One Man's Meat*, essays by E.B. White; Tilbury House Publishers, 1997.

p. 178: Edwin Way Teale quoted in *Walden Pond: A History*.

p. 185-186: *Down the River*, by Edward Abbey; E. P. Dutton & Co., 1982.

About the Author

David Goodman

Tom Slayton was editor-in-chief of *Vermont Life* magazine for twenty-one years, and is now its editor emeritus. He is a past president of the International Regional Magazine Association. Prior to his association with *Vermont Life*, he was a reporter and editor for Vermont newspapers for twenty years. His book *Sabra Field:The Art of Place* was published in 1994 and republished in 2002. He is also the author of *The Beauty of Vermont*, published in 1998; *Finding Vermont: An Informal Guide to Vermont's Places and People*; and various magazine and newspaper articles. Mr. Slayton is a regular commentator for Vermont Public Radio. He is a member of the Green Mountain Club, the Appalachian Mountain Club, and the Four Thousand Footer Club of the AMC. He lives in Montpelier with his wife, Elizabeth.

Other Contributors

J. Parker Huber, foreword contributor, has been a lifelong student of Henry David Thoreau's life and travels. He is the author of *The Wildest Country: A Guide to Thoreau's Maine*, published by the Appalachian Mountain Club, and *Elevating Ourselves: Henry David Thoreau on Mountains*, Mariner Books, Houghton Mifflin. He lives in Brattleboro, Vermont.

Original illustrations for *Searching for Thoreau* are by **Ethan Slayton,** a freelance artist who lives in Burlington, Vermont. He has studied at the Maine College of Art in Portland and at the Joe Kubert School of Cartoon and Graphic Art. He is the son of the author.

Bridget Besaw whose images of a Maine wilderness guide poling along Thoreau's path and of Katahdin Lake are featured on the covers of *Searching for Thoreau*, is an award-winning photographer specializing in the environment and natural resources and advocating for their protection. She has created photo projects for organizations such as The Nature Conservancy, Maine Woods Forever, and The Maine Farmland Trust. She recently self-published *Wildness Within, Wildness Without: Exploring Maine's Thoreau-Wabanaki Trail*, a photo book with collected essays, including one by Tom Slayton.

JUN 0 9 2011